Sacred Magic
REVISED

Discover Occult Secrets That Are Thousands Of Years Old!

William Alexander Oribello

Global Communications/Inner Light Publications

SACRED MAGIC
REVISED

By William Alexander Oribello
Copyright © 2012 Global Communications/Inner Light Publications

Non-fiction—Metaphysics

Timothy Green Beckley: Editorial Director
Carol Rodriguez: Publishers Assistant
Tim Swartz: Associate Editor
Sean Casteel: Editorial Assistant
William Kern: Editorial Assistant

Published by:
GLOBAL COMMUNICATIONS/INNER LIGHT PUBLICATIONS
P.O. BOX 753
NEW BRUNSWICK, N.J. 08903

www.conspiracyjournal.com

The information in this booklet is based on the research and experience of the author. No supernatural, medical or other effects can be guaranteed. The practitioner is responsible for the practice of these techniques, according to their faith.

DEDICATION

I would like to give special thanks to the wonderful people who instructed and guided me to the path of finding The Magical Temple of Light during my youth: Mr. Alexander Silverberg, Delores Brown, Professor S.D. Pickens, and others who cannot be mentioned by name for various reasons.

Current inspiration and loving support, has been given to encourage me in producing this revised edition of Sacred Magic by very special friends: Dr. Bart Mitchell, Christina Sanders, Maria Romero, Carlton Davis, Wayne Robinson, Inez Schimmelpfenning, Dorothy Calcagno, and Timothy Green Beckley.

Also, special thanks is given to my wife, Gayra, who lovingly devoted many hours in editing and typesetting this work, and to my daughter, Olivia, for giving of her personal time in assisting the proof reading of this manuscript.

All honor is offered to Divine Mind and the Ascended Masters of Wisdom for inspiring the writing of this book.

ABOUT THE AUTHOR

Since 1965, William Alexander Oribello has taught thousands of people how to improve their life in every way, through the proper application of Mystical Sciences.

During childhood, he had many experiences which guided him to first hand encounters with both Inner Plane and Living Adepts of the Secret Wisdom.

Mr. Oribello has delivered thousands of lectures, and his writings have been studied by seekers of Truth around the world.

At the present time, Mr. Oribello is accepting a limited number of students and clients, for those who are ready to enter the Path of Higher Initiation into The Divine Mysteries and The Great Work.

If, after reading this book, you feel the inner guidance for further instruction, write a letter concerning your past studies/experiences and future aspirations. Mail your letter to the author in care of the publisher, at the address below:

William Alexander Oribello
c/o INNER LIGHT PUBLICATIONS
P.O. BOX 753
NEW BRUNSWICK, N.J.   08903

INTRODUCTION

THE MISSION OF THIS BOOK

As we stand at the threshold of the 21st. century, we learn by observation that some things never change: Nearly every human being is still asking the eternal questions of, "Where did I originate? What is my purpose in life? What reality awaits me in the unknown, beyond my present life? How can I control my own life in relation to outside influences?"

Some answers to these, and other questions will be found within the pages of "Sacred Magic". One book of paper and ink cannot possibly contain all wisdom. However, such a book as this will serve as a springboard to awaken certain potent faculties, hidden within the esoteric structure of every living creature, in all time, space and dimensions.

To gain the most from this book, it is suggested that you read it casually from cover to cover. Then Read it again slowly, taking the time to practice some (or all) of the techniques, depending on your surroundings and degree of privacy.

You will notice the usage of the term "God" throughout this book. This is because most of its readers will have a traditional religious background. However, in truth, the Supreme Being is Pure Cosmic Essence-manifesting as both masculine and feminine in our highest form of comprehension - Divine Mother as well as Heavenly Father. Such is the mission of this book: To demonstrate the oneness of magic and true religion, and to use this two-fold unity as a tool to make a better person and a better world.

Many well meaning, but misinformed people associate magic with something evil or forbidden. This is because of misguided religious leaders who try to keep the masses in the grip of fear and ignorance. But as one age passes into another, we find that many people are claiming their Divine Right to decide for themselves as to what or what not to do. We are entering the long awaited Aquarian Age of Enlightenment, and find that even in this epoch of modern technology, people are seeking for the roots of an ancient "Secret Wisdom" to control their own lives, have greater well beingness, more success and prosperity. People are returning to Magic.

Several thousand years ago, one of the oldest religions in the world was about to become established, an Ancient Religion of Magic was founded, in the part of our globe later known as Persia. A man known as Zoroaster founded this religion. Later, some of the keepers of his Esoteric Teachings migrated to the continent of Africa, and were known there as "the Medianites".

In the opening chapters of the Book of Exodus, we see how Moses was tutored in the Knowledge and Wisdom of Egypt. When Moses realized he was of Hebrew Origin, he tried to free his people. He failed and was exiled from Egypt, banished to his own fate as a drifter in the desert.

Moses found his true destiny when he met Jethro, the Priest of Median (A Magi Initiate) and married his daughter. After 40 years Moses received and experienced Divine realization as recorded in the incident of "the Burning Bush". Moses was a true master of this Religion of Magic. Moses returned to Egypt and was able, with his wisdom and power, to free his people from bondage.

This Ancient Religion of Magic was not dogmatic and not one of blind faith, but one that used hidden laws of nature and believed in Divine Mind within one and all things. They believed in using these hidden laws to improve humankind as long as it was in harmony with the Divine Master Plan for the highest good of all involved.

Three Magi visited Jesus and brought him gifts of Gold (symbolic of nobility of character), Frankincense (symbolic of Divine Wisdom), and Myrrh (symbolic of personal power and self-mastery). These three Magi were called Astrologers, Kings of the East (Advanced Initiates), but most commonly were called "Wise Men". Today these three souls are now members of the Cosmic Hierarchy, also known as the Ascended Masters of the Wisdom. This Religion of Magic is seen throughout the Holy Bible.

I will demonstrate how some modern religious practices, as well as new age groups who focus on the intellectual approach, use the roots of magic in their presentations and practices.

Several Christian Churches use candles, incantations, incense, hand gestures, and other practices. Many of these practices were borrowed from the Ancient Mysteries, the Religion of Magic. Some Charismatic Christians practice clapping and raising of hands to "Praise the Lord" to the beat of Gospel Music. This is similar to how the American Indians, the Voodoo and the "Whirling Dervishes", and other cultures practice magic.

Some New Age practices such as Yogic Chanting, Aromatherapy, Rebirthing and others have their roots in ancient and modern magic. The wise ones of old have recorded the effects of certain herbal combinations, incense, oils, candles and ect. They even used an advanced form of Hypnotism in their Initiation Rites, to free the initiate of subconscious blocks, so that their lives would be transformed into one of great power. This was similar to what is now called rebirthing. The ancient Magi also taught that "he who possessed the Power of the Spoken Word" was the greatest initiate. This reminds us of modern day "Yogic Chanting" and "Affirmations" .

These examples may seem strange to you, however, when your awareness is opened it will become apparent to you. All is one and one is all. Government, religion and magic started out the same way. They were all for the good and benefit of humankind. All these things are good, essentially, it is only the misuse of these things that have given them a bad name, (including religion).

1. THE SEVEN FOLD PATH TO POWER

Before we explore the Seven Fold Path, I will reveal the great foundation for success in all types of mystic and psychic development; It is deep breathing and relaxation. This practice has been referred to as "The Silence", "The Inner Temple of Prayer" and by many other terms. It is, simply stated, going within to the very center of our being by stilling the senses and relaxing the physical body. This is the supreme method for opening our inner awareness.

THE METHOD

Sit relaxed or lie down and become as comfortable as possible. Make sure you do this at a time when you will not be disturbed. If you should fall asleep it would be perfectly alright, however, it would be better to stay awake so you may be more aware of what is taking place within you.

Take several deep breaths as follows: Inhale to the count of six, and hold the breath to the count of three. Now exhale to the count of six, and hold the breath out to the count of three. Repeat this several times and then return to normal breathing.

Now think of your feet, consciously willing that your feet become relaxed. Continue thinking of your feet until you are satisfied that they are relaxed. Now you will think of each major part of your

9

body, one by one. You will consciously relax each area. For example, you will think of your legs up to the knees, your thighs up to the hips, your stomach and lower back, chest and upper back, hands and arms, shoulders and neck, face and head. This technique is the perfect beginning to all prayers and meditations. You must be in a state of relaxation to attain total inner awareness.

THE SEVEN FOLD PATH TO POWER

This path constitutes seven mental qualities which we develop for the purpose of opening our inner awareness to an advanced degree. They were revealed to me by a master teacher many years ago and are very powerful. They are as follows:

1. OBSERVATION
2. VISUALIZATION
3. CONCENTRATION
4. MEDITATION
5. DISCRIMINATION
6. CONTEMPLATION
7. ADORATION

We will now examine each of these seven qualities and techniques.

OBSERVATION

This means to take special notice of things which we see with our physical sight. For example, the average person looks at a long stem red rose and that's all they see. On the other hand, a person with a trained sense of observation can see how many thorns are on the stem, the stem's various shades of green, the minute shades within the color of the rose, how each petal is shaped and more.

When you develop observation you not only see an object but you will truly know it. The more you observe yourself in thinking and actions the more you will know who you really are.

HOW TO DEVELOP OBSERVATION

Practice by noticing small details about different people and objects. Become more aware of events happening around you.The most important practice is to become more aware of your mental thought processes. What thoughts are going through your mind? What messages are you receiving?

VISUALIZATION

A great form of mental magic is to visualize what you desire as already accomplished in your mind. Simply stated, visualization is forming a perfect picture of your desire. You visualize this picture until you can actually feel your desire manifested into reality.

HOW TO DEVELOP VISUALIZATION

Begin your practice of visualization by becoming totally relaxed. Then begin to form a perfect mental picture of what you wish to accomplish. Add extra details until this picture is exactly what you want. Feel the joy of receiving the answer to your prayers. Visualization is, in fact, a form of dynamic prayer. Next is the most important step in your practice. Release the picture. Don't worry about how it will come about or when. Just release it to the Universe. Stop your practice now and do something else. Forget about it until your next session. You will find it will become easier to obtain your desires if you do the practices as instructed.

I would like to explain why releasing your perfected picture is one of the most important parts of visualization. It is based on a sound metaphysical principle. If you think about your desire constantly this causes you to hold it down to this level of limitation. You will think of so many ways of why and how it is impossible to obtain. However, when you release your perfected visualization, you turn it over to the all powerful Cosmic Mind. Your desires may come at an unexpected time and in an unexpected way. You should release and trust in the all wise and knowing "Higher Power". That Universal Power, will then transform your perfected picture into material opportunities. Your response to these opportunities will determine how quickly your desires will be manifested

CONCENTRATION

Your practice for concentration also includes visualization. You will begin by visualizing and then try to generate all of your energy into your one object of thought. This is concentration and if you can do this for as little as thirty seconds you have achieved a great deal. The mind loves to wander and flutter from thought to thought. In true concentration one does not force the mind to be still, but to run through its course of thoughts for several moments, after which it will begin to slow down. It is when your mind slows down that you can zero in with your practices of concentration. When you can master the art of concentration you will be able to accomplish many things in your daily life as well as inner awareness.

HOW TO DEVELOP CONCENTRATION

Use this exercise to help you develop your power of concentration. See yourself in front of a blackboard with a piece of chalk in one hand and an eraser in the other. Write the letters of the alphabet, one by one, on the blackboard. Use your eraser to erase each letter before you write the next one. If your mind wanders just gently bring your attention back to what you are doing. Start by working one third or halfway through the alphabet and then increase the time span until you have used all twenty six letters. You may then begin using numbers with this same method. Begin with the number one and go through to twenty five. Extend this until you can count to one hundred.

MEDITATION

The word meditate means to think quietly or to reflect. You can see how meditation is a part of concentration, visualization and observation. Meditation is often used to replace the word prayer. In fact, it is a prayer. Here is another explanation of meditation. Meditation is to consider all you know about an object or person. You then create a void within your mind so that you can receive more impressions and information about the object of your meditation.

HOW TO DEVELOP MEDITATION

Sit down at a table with pen and paper. You will now write down the object of your meditation. List every detail about what you already know of the subject. Now write out the fact that you want to know more. Place a dark colored cloth on the table and then place your paper on top of the table in front of you. Now go into a mental state of silence by bringing deep relaxation to your physical body. (See description for this practice on page 9 and 10). Open your eyes and place your elbows on the table. Cup your hands and place them around your forehead and eyes. Do this as if you are trying to shut out any distractions. The dark cloth and the cupping of your hands help you to focus your total attention on the paper. After you have considered your subject, create a mental void by closing your eyes as though your eyelids were a wall or curtain. See this curtain come down between your perception and the object of your meditation. During the few moments following the void is when you will receive your impressions from a higher consciousness, which will inform you and guide you in reference to your object. Be patient and remember that practice makes perfection.

In order to understand how this method really works you should also understand what is known as Sympathetic Attraction. You and every other person in the cosmos are linked together mentally. This means that all minds can affect other minds. If you pick up negative energy from other minds, it is because you are allowing yourself to be negative at this time. In other words you attract other thoughts which are sympathetic to your own. The ancients embodied this concept in the axiom, "Like attracts like". By the same principle you can attract more positive inspiration from illuminated minds. It is only your lack of awareness of the Cosmic Mind which blocks your path. By constant practice you begin to break the barriers, then you develop a rapport with all other minds of power and thus become attuned to God's mind.

DISCRIMINATION

Discrimination means non-attachment and indifference. This does not imply that you should be cold or insensitive, but that you should consider the true value of things you desire and their illusions. You have to discriminate between the real and the unreal. You must know what is the most important things in your life and if they are indeed for your highest good. In other words know what your priorities are.

HOW TO DEVELOP DISCRIMINATION

Use this practice to increase you power of discrimination. Make a general list of all your present activities and desires. Then consider each one, asking yourself, "Is this matter really important in a cosmic sense?". If the inner answer is no, then mark a line through this item and try to eliminate it from your life and your consciousness. The key to this practice is to simplify your life by discarding all unimportant things.

CONTEMPLATION

Contemplation means to look at or think about something with deep thought. Look at the subject with an over all view type attitude. Information will come to you easily when you attain the contemplative state of thinking.

15

HOW TO DEVELOP CONTEMPLATION

There are many things you will want to contemplate about. Events or emotional feelings about your childhood, your young adult life, your current life and your future. This is a practice you may use for a number of reasons. It will help you to release negative feelings and be more positive. Remember you can't change past events but you can gain understanding and learn from them. Now begin this practice by sitting at a table with a lit candle in front of you. At first just sit and contemplate the candle flame and allow your mind to relax. Now you will want to focus upon your chosen subject. Visualize it embodied within the flame. If you are trying to release a negative fixation about the subject you should visualize a positive aspect replacing the negative. Contemplate on how to change it. If you are trying to gain understanding you should ask for insight of the subject. Most past experiences that are painful are from lack of understanding or lack of forgiveness. You will find many ways to use this practice to help yourself.

ADORATION

When you have developed along the path to a more advanced stage of contemplation you will begin to fall in love with the beauty of life. You will begin to see beyond the general appearance of people and things. You will then possess the ability to see the true essence of life and behold the face of God in everything and everyone. At this stage you begin to live in a state of grace. You will also find that the will of God becomes clear and great expectations of miracles flow.

Ugliness turns into beauty, sorrow turns
into joy and hate turns into love. This
is truly a state of knowing who you are.

HOW TO DEVELOP ADORATION

Take time to notice the things around
you. Look at the beauty of nature. Gaze
at the sunrise and the sunset. The birds,
the flowers and most important look within your own being. Realize you are a part
of the great cosmic plan. You are a most
powerful being. You are learning how to
become one with all there is.

As you practice the Seven-Fold Path to
Power you will truly know yourself. You
will discover by using these techniques
that your true inner awareness will give
you great peace and joy.

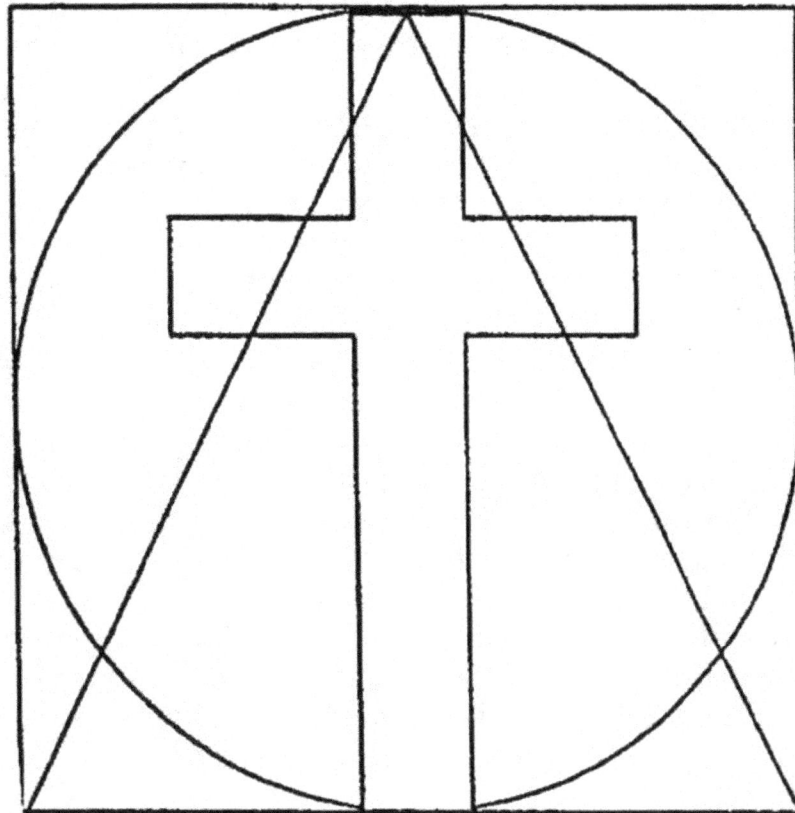

2. MAGICAL PROTECTION

As you follow the Seven-Fold Path to
Power, you will come across other matters
and areas of your life that will call for
added information. You will need to learn
more in order for you to master these
matters. You are a multi-dimensional
being. In this book I will give you the
wisdom and insight to cover all these
areas of your life. I also will give you
the necessary tools to overcome the fears
and complexes you have developed in this
incarnation as well as past incarnations.
In this chapter I will instruct you in
the art of magical self-defense. You may
ask why you would need self-defense in
spiritual matters. It would not only be
self-defense but also self-preservation.

As you know, when you start to practice
these truths, your life will become more
joyous and happy. People will start to be
jealous of your progress. They may even
ask you to help them but may not be as
willing to work hard like you have. This
is why you may wish to keep your work a
secret. Telling people too much about
your secret work can open you to receive
bad luck or a curse against you. Yes, I
know this may seem a little far out. You
may think that being hexed or cursed is
the work of an over active imagination.
You may think that only a person that is
unstable or wants to blame his or her
troubles on someone else are the only
people that would believe in such things.

Let us look at the principles involved.

18

As you have learned, you can create with the power of your mind. This also applies to people that wish you harm: Negative emotions are usually very strong and very powerful. For example, when one is angry, it seems easy to release this negativity with an outburst of angry energy. If you do not protect yourself, you can leave yourself wide open to such vibrations, both expressed and/or silent. This is why you will have to be more careful when you begin your work. Now I will give you the ways in which these harmful emotions can affect you and how you can use magical protection to help yourself.

WHAT IS A CURSE?

An enemy may wish bad luck on your life and plans. They hold negative thoughts to the effect that you will become ill, lose your mind, fail at business and personal relationships, be unhappy and a host of many other possible calamities. They can focus this energy against you a number of different ways. It may be for a number of petty reasons, such as jealousy, or not wanting you to be with someone or being a rivalry on your job. To put it simply, a curse is a negative energy. It may lodge itself in your mind forming a negative obsession, or a deeply rooted emotional problem. It could manifest in your body as an unnatural pain or condition. It can cause you to have accidents or to drop things, forget important things, lack of interest or attention about important matters, become easily upset, lose your self confidence, or hate others and a host of other negative feelings. I will now expose several ways by which an evil person may send a curse upon you.

19

INTIMIDATION

When someone constantly tries to insult or make you look bad in front of others it may be that the person is using this evil technique to curse you. Such people may do this in a joking way, but this has a certain effect on you that makes you feel cornered, helpless and embarrassed. Beware of such people and separate from them if it is possible. If you cannot, take the person aside and tell them that you insist they stop intimidating you. If they refuse to stop, the only thing left to do is to tell them off openly for their lack of consideration. The reason this is so important is because when a person constantly, and deliberately intimidates you, they are trying to break down your mental and emotional shield. This opens you up to their negative forces. In order for a negative magic spell to take effect, the victim's confidence must be weakened in some way.

Another method of intimidation used by evil workers, is to place a gum like substance in the victim's path by an unclean substance. This may be in the form of grave yard dirt or some other unclean matter. You may think this is really using a wild imagination, but believe me there are people that use these methods and more. If you have developed your power of observation you will notice such things. To be informed is to be protected. I will now explain how this one practice can work. You pick up the dust on your shoes by means of the gum. This may even cause you to trip or fall because the evil worker has placed their negative wishes into this dust. In this way the sorcerer is given an open door into your field of energy.

Another example of intimidation is the display of ill omens. The worker of evil places this ill omen in front of your door or on your property in an obvious place. It could be a dead black cat, a mouse, black roses or other ill omens.

You will need to know how the law of sympathetic magic works in order to be fully protected. Here is how this magic is used against you; Every human being radiates a magnetic energy field known as the aura. Through contact with parts of the victim's body such as nail clippings, hair, blood, saliva, or clothing the evil worker makes contact. Our emotional and mental energy, our physical vitality, our very life is contained within our auric force field. When a strand of hair, a nail clipping or ect. is separated from our body a portion of our life force remains on that part for a certain amount of time. Through such an item a spiritual worker can help you or an evil sorcerer can place a curse on you. One way the evil worker can harm you is by using a portion of your body to attach to a voodoo doll. They then place the doll in a fire, stick pins in it, or even suspend it with a string around its neck. While they are doing this they are placing their evil intent against you. This is why I mentioned earlier in this chapter; Angry negativity can be used against you whether it be expressed or silent. The above is the silent type of curse. I will now give you more insight on how highly emotional out bursts can affect you.

When someone becomes angry and blurts

out a highly emotional expression, such words become thought forms which grow stronger with time. The person to whom the words were directed may find they are under a curse which can only be broken if they overcome the trait which angered the other person. Some people are under curses which have followed them into many lives or incarnations. I will reveal how one can free themselves from curses such as these as we progress.

HOW TO PREVENT A CURSE

Try not to offend anyone if there is any way to avoid it. At times it is impossible to avoid offending someone because some people have peculiar ways. However, just to be mindful of their feelings will make it easier to have harmony.

In some cases your enemies are those who were once considered friends but a negative thing happened between you. Over the years, I have met many people who think they have many friends, only to find out in hard times that they were not as many as they thought. You may have a number of relationships that are casual and friendly, but this does not mean they are your true friend. A true friend is someone that will stand with you in all circumstances.

Friendship cannot be bought, nor can it be forced upon anyone. It is something that develops between two people who are attracted to each other by the means of one or several common interests. In order to have more harmony between you and another you should follow these most important tips.

22

1. Don't compromise your individuality.
You are important. Do not try to change
yourself in order to make someone your
friend. This never works out.

2. Be considerate of others. If you are
doing or saying anything which offends
the other person, then stop saying or
doing it. Always try to put yourself in
the other person's place.

3. If others offend you. Tell them as
soon as you are given the opportunity.
You do not have to get angry before you
tell them. If a person is really a friend
they will appreciate your honesty.

4. Take time to listen. Really listen
when others are talking. Many people hear
but do not listen. This is one of the
most common causes for misunderstandings.

5. If others become your enemy. You have
to release them in love and forgiveness.
One way to do this is to write a letter
to the person. Express all of your hurts
and resentments. Then burn the letter and
say out loud, "I forgive and release you
in cosmic love and light". This is a safe
way to release your negative feelings
toward the person. Holding on to negative
feelings can harm you. You may have to do
the above practice more that one time in
order to receive peace.

6. Don't fight back. This puts you on
their level of negativity. This will only
cause you to attract more negative people
and more negative situations. Remember
this always, "Like attracts like".

7. Control your anger. Do not allow a

person to arouse your anger to the point of an outburst. Just as angry negativity can affect you, you can harm yourself by releasing your anger in this way. I will now share a great truth with you. It is not what a person says to you that angers you. It is what you think about what the person said to you, that angers you.

PRACTICAL TECHNIQUES
FOR PERSONAL PROTECTION

An enemy can hinder your progress by the look of envy, known as The Evil Eye. This is an age old belief. In Italian legends it is known as the Molochia (pronounced Moloykee). It has also been called the Overlooks. The concept behind this belief is that one can place a curse or hindrance upon another through the gaze. It is not the actually gaze but the thought behind the gaze that propels the curse.

The eyes are a treasured possession, the windows of the soul. This light reveals the true personality. The eyes are very powerful and through the gaze, they can reveal the inner thoughts of a person.

Use the following method of protection when you feel a person looking at you with an evil gaze. Look at that person right between their eyes. While you are doing this try to generate love as you say in your mind, "You cannot hurt me". They will have to look away from you.

Here is another method of protection against the Evil Eye. Use the thumb of the hand that you write with, and make the Sign of the Cross on the top of your head. Then repeat the following words:

"Sanct Matheus, Sanct Marcus, Sanct Lucas Sanct Johannis". Do this practice for a total of three times. These words are pronounced as follows: The "a" in the word Sanc, is pronounced as in the word "arrow". This is the same in all four benedictions. Matheus: Math is like in the word "mathematics"; the "e" is said like an "a" as in the word "cake"; "us" is like in the word "us". Marcus: Mar is said like the "mar" in the word "market"; "cus" as in the word "custard". Lucas: Lu, the "u" sounds like the "oo" in the word "moon"; Cas is like the "cas" in the word "castle". Johannis: Jo is said like the name "Joe"; Hann is like the "hann" in the name "Hanna"; Is as in the word "pistol".

   The method I will give you now is used as a protective shield. You will wear it on the left side of your body because you receive negative vibrations from this side.

   You can prepare this symbol on a small piece of white paper, however, sincere practitioners choose to use parchment. They also use a quill pen and Dove's Blood Brand ink. You can obtain these items from your local occult/metaphysical shop.

   Write the arrangement of letters as the diagram shown below.

```
             I.
          N.I.R.
             I.
      SANCTUS SPIRITUS
             I.
          N.I.R.
             I.
```

25

The letters I.N.R.I. often appear at the top of a Crucifix and represent the first letters of Hebrew words for the four elements. The four elements are air, fire, water and earth. The four arms of the cross represent the limitations imposed by the physical existence (the four elements) upon the soul of man. The words "Sanctus Spiritus" means Holy Spirit. This symbol of letters signifies that you receive power to overcome blocks through and by the Divine Spirit.

Once you have copied the symbol, you should wrap it in cloth and wear it pinned to your clothing on the left side.

Another powerful protection symbol, using words arranged in a certain order, is the Sator Square. This symbol was discovered carved on stone, written on scrolls and engraved on talismans.

Copy the words below. Again you may use a small piece of white paper but it is suggested that you use parchment, a quill pen and Dove's Blood brand ink.

```
SATOR
AREPO
TENET
OPERA
ROTAS
```

This diagram is also wrapped in cloth or put into a red cloth bag which has a drawstring at the top. These bags are also available at your local occult shop. You wear it pinned to your clothing on the left side.

The Sator Symbol has been interpreted to mean "the beginning and the end". The beginning of the Lord's Prayer has been found hidden within this powerful symbol.

The word Sator means "to sow" or to do our deeds. It is associated with the spiritual power of the Planet Saturn, the giver of discipline and karma. Therefore, you are asking for help to make your way easier, so that you can learn lessons through inner spiritual inspiration rather than by unfortunate experiences.

The word Arepo means "to plow" or reap the harvest of our deeds. Therefore, you are appealing to "the Lords of Karma", which are over your personal progress. You are asking assistance through your personal spirit guides.

The word Tenet means to "believe", or hold certain tenets of philosophical or religious belief. You are affirming your belief in a higher power to assist you in your daily life.

The word Opera means "the act" or the drama of an individual life. You are seeing that through your daily works and dramas are the lessons that can awaken you to higher knowledge.

Rotas means "the wheel" or the return of our actions to teach us lessons. You are realizing that life is a continuous wheel. By remembering our past and present experiences, both good and bad, you gain wisdom. You must do this with no resentment, pain or attachment.

The Sator Symbol has been used in a number of different ways. I have shown you a way to use it for your own personal protection and power.

A simple way to protect yourself is to use blessed salt and red pepper on your shoes. Use a new box of table salt, or sea salt if available, say a prayer over it. Be sincere and use your own words. Mix one part red pepper and three parts of the blessed salt. Put some of this on the outside back part of each shoe. You should do this before leaving your home so you can be protected in your steps each day.

PRACTICAL TECHNIQUES TO PROTECT YOUR HOME

To protect your home and keep evil away, you should put the herb, nettle, in front of every doorway inside your home.

You may also place mustard seeds on top of doorways and window sills.

Another method is by the sprinkling of blessed salt. You may use the same method to bless the salt that I gave you on this page, under Personal Protection. Sprinkle some blessed salt into all of the corners of your home. Once a month you should vacuum or sweep the salt, dispose of it and replace it with new salt.

TECHNIQUES TO PROTECT YOUR LOVED ONES

You may use this technique to protect your loved ones, including your friends, your family and your pets.

Use the practices you have learned to put yourself in a state of relaxation. You will use your power of imagination to visualize a stream of light coming from your forehead, between your eyes. Then see this light totally surrounding your loved one. Visualize the light in the form of a large bubble surrounding them. Repeat the following affirmation: "I send the light of love and peace to you. I place this circle of light around for your protection against all harm and so it is". Now release your work to the Higher Powers. You may repeat this method whenever you feel it is needed.

TECHNIQUES TO PROTECT YOUR POSSESSIONS

You should use the bubble of light method to protect your possessions. This includes your personal possessions as well as your automobile. This can keep you protected against accidents and/or robbery.

THE ULTIMATE TECHNIQUE FOR PROTECTION

Always remember that the greatest and most powerful form of protection comes from within you. To keep a positive mind and think only the highest thoughts of goodwill and harmony will keep you from harm. However, to stay strong mentally emotionally, and spiritually is not always possible. In our daily lifes of co-existing with others, we experience outside influences. This can put us in a weakened state. The first thing to do is to use some type of self-protection each day. The second thing you should do is to simplify your life by having positive influences around you. Try to avoid all types of negativity.

3. THE KEY TO NATURE'S SECRETS

The information in this chapter was imparted to me by several wise ones; Holy men and women who have mastered many secrets of the universe. I have tried these things and found them to be effective in my own life.

RESTFUL SLEEP

Correct sleeping is very important to your health and well being. Before going to sleep, you should clear your mind of all negative thoughts and totally relax in the following manner: Lie down and take several deep breaths, hold the breath each time for just a moment and then exhale slowly through the nose. Relax, with each breath that you take, and think that all tension, worry and anger are leaving you. Breathe slowly now. Mentally withdraw the tension from every part of your body by thinking of your toes, your feet, your legs, and so forth. When you have reached your chest then start thinking of your hands, arms and shoulders. Then your neck, face and entire head. This is a wonderful exercise to relax the entire body.

POWER OF HERBS

Herbs have been used for many thousands of years to promote health and prolong youth. Consider the following list of herbs and their uses:

Anise gives a stimulating effect to the

mind and body. To use-inhale the aroma of Anise.

Canada Snake Root and Wood Betony taken as a tea can be of great help in cases of extreme nervousness.

Cheese plant leaves and Corn Silk tea are taken frequently to help with bladder and kidney problems.

Cloves are used for an aromatic inhaler. Take a small jar of vaseline and sprinkle it with cloves, eucalyptus and mint leaves. Mix well then apply to the tip of your finger and inhale the aroma.

Dandelion leaves are used as a remedy for low blood pressure. Drink as a tea.

Dandelion Root and Yarrow Herb are taken in the form of a tea to help keep diabetes in check.

Dandelion Root and Rhubarb Root are taken as a tea for liver conditions.

Garlic or Valerian Root tea is used to reduce High Blood Pressure.

Ginseng is the best means of prevention of illness and disease. It is wise to make sure you use the finest quality of Ginseng. The root extract is the most recommended form.

Golden Seal Herb Tea is said to cause a distaste for alcohol, therefore being helpful in overcoming alcoholism.

Lavender relieves headaches that are due to fatigue. To use-drink lavender tea.

Lily of the Valley and Lobelia used as a tea to improve heart conditions.

Pumpkin seed gives one vigor, virility, and regeneration. To use-eat the seeds.

Red Clover Blossom and Violet Leaf tea are used to combat cancer.

Wild Plum Bark and Lobelia Herb tea usually brings relief for people with Asthma.

A proven cure for hiccups is to apply the the following: Take some water in your mouth but do not swallow it. Next you must plug your ears with your fingers so that you cannot hear anything. Then you would swallow the water. Do this three to four times in succession. If it does not stop, repeat the procedure after five minutes.

A very effective cure for loss of voice due to a cold or strain, is to eat lemon peels. Wash a fresh lemon in warm water, remove the peel and eat it. Chew it thoroughly before swallowing.

Treatment for the common cold is to use the following remedy at the first sign of the cold. Place a teaspoon of baking soda in a glass of water and drink. Do this four times within a twenty-four hour period.

Natural vitamins can also be a great source to sustain health and youth. You can obtain natural vitamins and herbs at your local health food store. You can check the Yellow Page section of your local telephone directory for one in your area. If you find your area does not have such a store, you can obtain these herbs and vitamins through the mail. A good mail order store is Penn Herb Co.,The address is 603 North 2nd. St., Phila., PA 19123-3098.

GREAT REALIZATION

Much of humanity is in an illusion and they call this illusion reality. This is the cause for most of the suffering on this planet. One of the greatest of man's illusions is the belief that we need so many things and luxuries in order to be happy. A great adept revealed to me the four things that constitute existence of life on this planet. These four things are free. You do not buy them but you are responsible for the survival of them. They are as follows:

Air-One of the most precious things necessary to survival on this planet. Without it one cannot breathe and without breath the human physically dies. How many of us realize the importance of air? We pollute it every day with our inventions of progress(?) and it is becoming a rare thing to be able to take a breath of fresh air. We say we need more, more, more of this and more of that. We build more factories, produce more cars so they can continue to poison our precious air. What a dear price to pay for more of what we think we need.

Water-The human body is composed mostly of water. Through the spending of energy and the passing of time, the cells of our body are going through a change of dying and being replaced. If we do not take in the proper materials (and in their proper quantity) the cells are not replaced as they should be and illness may set in. Water has, like our air, also been ruined and polluted through dumping of poison waste matter from factories, and other inventions of man.

RICH SOIL-Rich Soil is a great necessity because from it we grow our food. Again, there are newer techniques of agriculture being used to grow things but somewhere down the line a compromise is being made that brings about a lack of quality. I hear people say all the time that things don't taste as good as they used to.

OIL-Last, but not least, we will consider oil. The adept told me a reason for the oil that flows in the depths of the earth. Its purpose is a simple matter of hydraulics. The layers of the earth's crust are not stationary as it appears, but they are shifting. The oil makes it all move easier. So we come to understand that oil has an overall purpose to the earth. It is not just for mans use of modern inventions and to run machinery.

Much of humanity is in an illusion. We worry more about unimportant matters, not realizing the the very foundation of life on our planet is in danger. There are some organizations trying to make people aware of this danger. They are trying to save mother earth. However, until people as a whole begin to look at others as a part of themselves and at humanity as a family, will the answers come. When we all walk in harmony hand in hand regardless of race, color, or creed will we discover the greatest secret of peace and survival, and that is working together and manifesting the word,"Love".

Take time each day to visualize God's light around our planet and pray for all the people that inhabit mother earth. Do this before you go to sleep each night. You will find it is worth the effort.

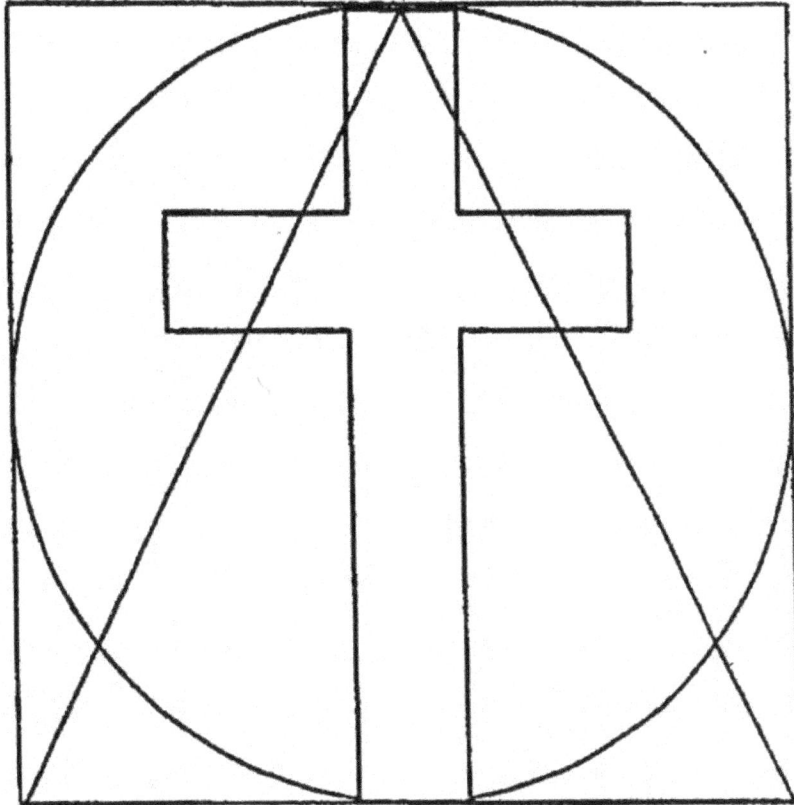

4. STONES, COLORS, AND CANDLES

You will find when working with Sacred Magic some will call these practices just superstition. Some may think you are a little unstable and some may even think you are evil. This stems from a lack of understanding. I will now explain that which is termed superstition. This will give you a better understanding of the principles involved in this work.

There are things we see every day that we call reality, things believed to be based on facts. We are considering the difference between factual realities and superstition. We obviously understand factual realities but do not understand superstition. The difference between the two is the limit of our understanding. We must remind ourselves that what we believe to be reality, in some cases, cannot be seen, felt or heard. For example, we cannot see, hear or feel our thoughts but we know that we think. We know there are sounds that we cannot see, hear, or feel such as radio/tv sound waves. Here is another example. Before the introduction of radio, people would have thought it impossible. They were so amazed. "A talking box?", I know that if it had been discovered years earlier, the inventor would have been condemned as a sorcerer and would have been burned up along with his "Magic Talking Box". This can apply to many things today, with so many new inventions. I just wish to open your understanding to the possibilities of the higher side of life.

Superstitions begin to fade as we are given the understanding behind the hidden symbolism. Superstition then becomes reality to us based on the knowledge of the laws at work in them.

MYSTIC STONES

I will now share valuable information concerning the mystic properties and use of certain stones.

LOADSTONES-It is said that to wear one of these stones on each side of your body, will balance your magnetic power. They are also used to draw out and neutralize negative conditions in healing work.

TIGER'S EYE-Use this stone to attract health, happiness and prosperity. If rubbed on the eyelids it is said to improve eyesight.

LAPIS LAZULI (AZURE)-This stone is kept for universal harmony with divine cosmic love. Used also for psychic protection.

AMETHYST-Used to bring honor and soberness of mind. It repels evil influences. When worn to bed it brings pleasant dreams and a good night's rest.

MOONSTONE-It is said to preserve youth. Used to open the faculties for enchanted memories and prophecy when placed between the eyes. Also, brings peace of mind and inner security.

CRYTALS-These valuable gems of nature are composed of the highest vibration of

condensed matter, able to contain the
program of creation itself from the
Universal Mind. Crystals can store and
channel energy. Because crystals are
amplifiers for any energy programmed into
them, they can be used as a tool to
enchance the energy in your magical work.
One may breathe their visualizations into
a crystal and enhance the power of that
thought. One may intone a chant into a
crystal and amplify its power many times.
To develop psychic powers, place on a
black cloth and then place a lit candle
several inches to the left of the
crystal. Then you would gaze into the
crystal.

COLOR MAGIC

I will now discuss colors. Following is
the seven colors of the spectrum with
their mystical properties explained.

1. **Red** is a stimulating color. It is
connected with love, awakening, and
passion. It corresponds to the element of
earth.

2. **Orange** is associated with the sunset
and has a healing effect on the nerves.
It corresponds to the element of water.

3. **Yellow** is associated with sunlight and
stimulates the emotions. it corresponds
to the element of fire.

4. **Green** is associated with development
and has a peaceful effect. It corresponds
to the element of air.

5. **Light Blue** is a healing color. Its
vibration has a calming effect. It also

38

indicates spirituality. It corresponds to the etheric substance.

6. Dark Blue is the color of high spiritual attainment. it corresponds to higher mental substance.

7. Violet is the color of the highest spirituality. It corresponds to the spirit made manifest.

CANDLE MAGIC

The human mind associates darkness with the unknown and with limitation. There is something about light that makes anything seem more inviting and promising to the average mind.

Since early times, man has used fire as a tool of prayer. The flame symbolized the Light of Divine Mind, giving hope and energy to the subject of meditation. Many practitioners use candles in the art of praying with fire.

In candleburning rituals, one focuses their attention on the flame as a doorway through which they communicate their desires to the higher dimensions. It is within the higher planes that the energy of the practitioner, together with the energy of intelligent forces, becomes a dynamo that manifests in this dimension as a turn of events, new opportunities, etc.

It has been a practice to use different color candles for different purposes. I will now give a list of these.

White Candles-Spiritual Communion, used

generally in prayer. It is also believed that to burn white candles in behalf of earthbound souls, sheds light on their path.

Black Candles-Used to overcome crossed conditions, absorb evil vibrations out of, and away from the practitioner.

Blue Candles-Used for healing, peace and psychic development.

Red Candles-Used for love attraction, and physical vitality.

Pink Candles-For friendship and harmony with others.

Orange Candles-Used to maintain physical balance, sooth nervous systems and for concentration.

Yellow Candles-Used to maintain emotional balance and for higher intelligence.

Green Candles-For money attraction, good fortune and for business.

Purple Candles-For spiritual attainment and personal power.

You can obtain the different color candles from your local occult supply shop. However, if it is not possible to obtain color candles, you may use a white candle for all your needs. White reflects all colors and is the color of purity. You will also need a good all purpose oil for blessing your candle. This is also available from your local shop. The following is how to consecrate the oil for blessing your candles.

HOW TO CONSECRATE OIL

Olive oil or All purpose oil may be used. Place some oil in a bowl in front of you. Now take several deep breaths as follows: Inhale to the count of six, and hold the breath to the count of three. Exhale to the count of six, and hold the breath out to the count of three. Repeat this several times. As you do this, you will concentrate on the energy that you are creating to be stored in your hands. Hold both hands over the bowl of oil. Now visualize a white light coming from your hands and going into the oil. See the white light pushing out and dissolving all negativity. As you see the bowl of oil becoming one with the white light, say the following: "I bless this oil to become a Holy Anointing Oil to bless my candles." Store the oil in a clean jar until you are ready to use it.

HOW TO CLEANSE AND BLESS CANDLES

To clean your candles. First rub them completely with mineral oil then rub the wicks with water. Wipe with a clean cloth and let set a few hours.

Blessing a candle is done one of two ways. This depends on the purpose, either attracting or repelling.

If you are blessing the candle to drive away or remove a negative condition, do the following: Take some of your blessed oil on your right thumb and first two fingers. Touch the center of the candle and rub it towards the bottom of the

41

candle, one time. Take more oil on the same fingers. Touch the same center spot of the candle and rub towards the top of the candle, one time. While you do this think of the undesirable condition going away from you. Below is a diagram of how to do this.

Blessing a Candle to Repel

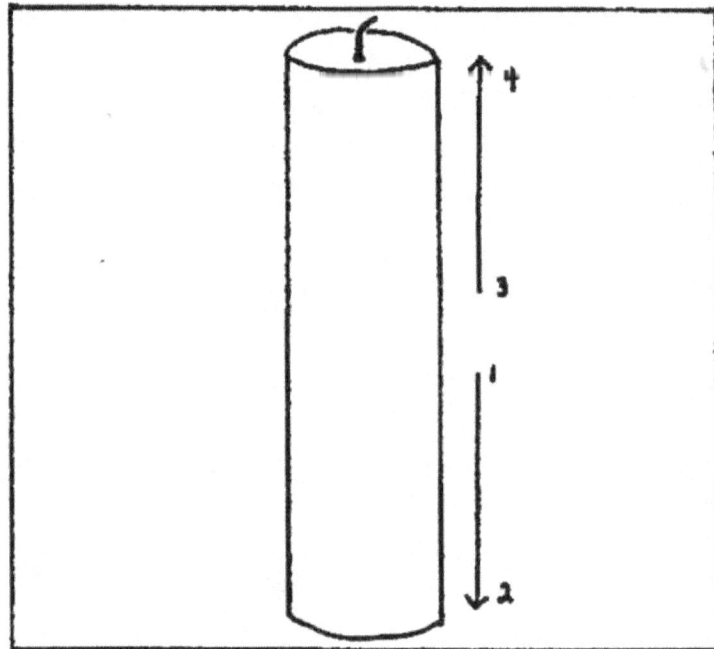

If you are blessing a candle to attract desired conditions do the following: Take some blessed oil on your right thumb and first two fingers. Touch the bottom of the candle and rub towards the center, one time. Take more oil on the same fingers and touch the top of the candle and rub towards the center, stopping at the same center spot. On the next page is a diagram to show you how to do this.

BLESSING A CANDLE TO ATTRACT

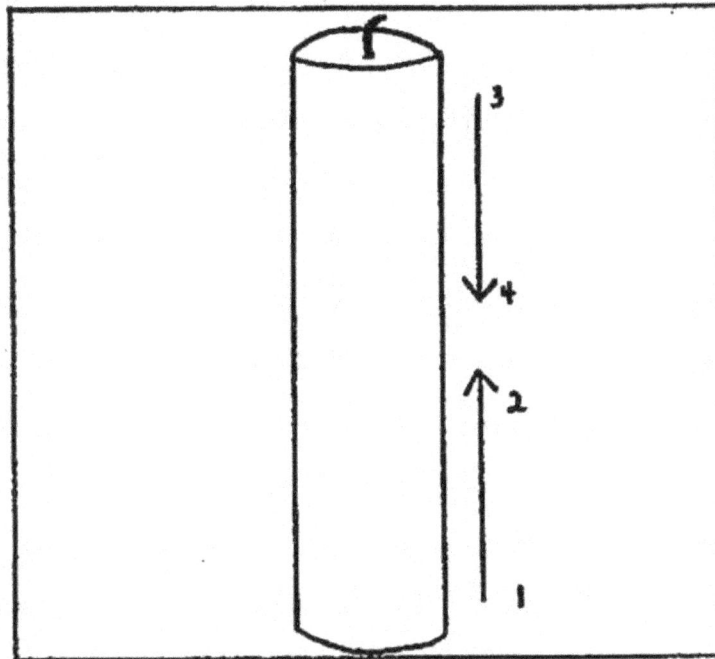

WHEN TO BURN CANDLES

If you are burning the candle for
yourself you must do so during your
mystic hour. To find your mystic hour,
simply add all the numbers in your
birthdate. If your date of birth, for
example, is 12-11-1944 you would add
1+2+1+1+1+9+4+4= 23. Since your answer is
not one of the two digit numbers on the
clock, you will have to reduce it to a
single digit, add 2+3= 5. Your mystic
hour would be 5 A.M. or 5 P.M. You may
burn your candle at either time or at
both times. If your first addition gives
you 10, 11, or 12 then that is your
mystic hour. If you have any other two
digit number, you will have to reduce it
to a single digit. If for someone else
you will use their date of birth.

5. THE NUMBER SECRET

For ages humankind has been fascinated by the obvious powers and mystical uses of numbers, each number has its own vibration. Each combination of numbers have their own vibration. The ancient philosophers knew this and used the power of numbers to work mystical practices. They also taught their students how to use numbers to calculate the best months, days, and even the best hours in which to begin a new project.

I will now reveal the symbolic meaning of each number with its alleged powers.

ONE-is the number of individuality. It represents God, the one universal mind in and around all there is. One represents the primal element, the one source of all life....The Beginning.

TWO-represents the duality within all things. It also is symbolic of the law of opposites such as heat and cold, day and night, positive and negative, ect.

THREE-is representative of the triune manifestation of Father, Son, and Holy Spirit: The trinity of time, when we consider time as past, present, and future. The three points of a triangle are symbolic of this number as time, space, and consciousness.

FOUR-is the number of a good foundation and balance. There are four corners of a house. Four seasons of the year which are

44

winter, spring, summer, and fall. There are four elements. They are earth, air, fire, and water. The four great virtues are patience, temperance, fortitude, and justice.

FIVE-has great mystic virtues for it is symbolic of uniting our duality with the power of the trinity; 2 + 3= 5. It also reveals the hint of the mystic formula for the regeneration of humankind. When we have accomplished balance and harmony between the duality of our being, natural and spiritual, we then become master of the three lower realms of existence. These levels are the physical, the emotional, and the mental. We then form the reflection or microcosm of the three-fold nature of God. There are five fingers on each hand, five toes on each foot, and five extremities of the body. The five extremities are two arms, two legs and the head.

SIX-is often referred to as the number of man, for it is written that man was created on the sixth day of creation. It is symbolic of the six pointed star known as The Star of David. The symbol of the six pointed star consists of two triangles, one pointing up (representing perfected man or the striving to perfection), and the other pointing down (representing the Divine reaching into our lives). This is the supreme accomplishment of the initiate - to unite the trinity of our being with the trinity of the Divine so that we may attain cosmic consciousness or oneness with the Universal Mind.

SEVEN-has been called the perfect or divine number. There are seven states of matter which manifest as the seven realms of existence; the seven-fold man; seven spirits of God before His throne; the book of seven seals; seven life waves; the seven stars; and seven symbolic churches of the book of Revelation; the seven energy centers of the etheric body.

EIGHT-is the number of universal harmony, for it symbolizes the axiom, "As above, So below" by its appearance of two circles, one atop the other. It has been called the number of Jesus, The Christ, and also the number of regenerated man who has attained harmony and oneness with the higher life.

NINE-is also called a perfect number because of the thirty three symbolism; Jesus is said to have lived on earth for 33 years after which he completed his mission. There are 33 degrees of study in some of the wisdom schools. The 33 must be multiplied as 3 x 3 = 9. In this arcane formula man accomplishes the perfection of his three lower bodies, the three higher bodies, and unites them with the three-fold aspect of Divinity.

TEN-is the number of completion. One is the beginning or alpha; Zero is the ending or omega. This makes ten the number of the completed work or the creation, the Kabbalistic Yod.

THE MYSTIC 9 - GOOD & EVIL

Here is some additional information concerning the number nine. It is the number of the human path of wisdom for either good or evil. For instance, in the thirteenth chapter of the Book of Revelation we are told about the Anti

46

Christ and the Mark of the Beast. We are
told that the Number of the Beast is
related to man and the number is 666. Now
if you add these numbers thus you have
the number 18; 6 + 6 + 6 =18. When you
add 1 + 8 you have 9. This means that
this is the evil path of wisdom or the
carnal knowledge which most humans cling
to.

In the next chapter of Revelation, we
are told of the righteous people of God
on Mount Zion. Their number is 144,000.
Again, if we add these numbers we come
out with nine, 1+4+4+0+0+0= 9. This is
symbolic of the sacred path of wisdom or
the spiritual knowledge of regenerated
man.

MAGIC IN YOUR NAME

Your name contains your own mystic
number which you can use in various ways
to help yourself. I wish to explain that
there are only nine numbers. Any number
beyond nine is just a combination of
numbers. For example 12 is a combination
of 1 and 2. In all work regarding numbers
the combination must be added together to
produce a single digit number.

Now I will show you how to receive your
mystic number from the vibration of your
name. Using the chart below you will
notice the letters of the Alphabet listed
under the numbers 1 through 9.

1	2	3	4	5	6	7	8	9
A	B	C	D	E	F	G	H	I
J	K	L	M	N	O	P	Q	R
S	T	U	V	W	X	Y	Z	

It is very simple to find your mystic

name number. I will explain by way of an example. I will use the name John Henry Smith to demonstrate. J = 1, O = 6, H = 8, N = 5. Add the numbers for the first name, John, 1 + 6 + 8 + 5= 20. Reduce 20 down to 2 (2 + 0= 2). This means that John vibrates to the number 2. Now take the name Henry. H = 8, E = 5, N = 5, R = 9, and Y = 7. Add the numbers for Henry, 8 + 5 + 5 + 9 + 7= 34. Reduce 34 down to 7, (3 + 4= 7). Henry vibrates to the number 7. Now find the numbers for Smith. S = 1, M = 4, I = 9, T = 2, and H = 8. Add the numbers for Smith, 1 + 4 + 9 + 2 + 8 = 24. Reduce 24 to 6, (2 + 4= 6). Smith vibrates to the number 6.

Now you will add the three numbers of the name together. John=2, Henry=7 and Smith=6, now you have 15, (2+7+6=15). Reduce 15 to 6, (1 + 5= 6). This persons name number is 6.

At this stage we will find the person's birth number. This is obtained by adding the day, month and year of birth. For example, let us say John Henry Smith was born on November 17th., 1934. Since it is the 11th. month, the 17th day, and year 1934, you would add like this; 1 + 1 + 1 + 7 + 1 + 9 + 3 + 4= 27. Reduce 27 to 9, (2 + 7= 9). So the birth number would be 9.

Next I will show you how to determine the number of destiny of a person. To find this you just add the name number which is 6 and the birth number which is 9,(6 + 9= 15). Reduce 15 to 6, (1+5= 6). So the number of destiny is 6.

You now have the name, birth and destiny number for our example, John

48

Henry Smith. If John wanted to find his
best three digit number for any purpose,
it would be 696. If he wanted a single
digit, he would just add 6+9+6=21. Reduce
21 to 3, (2+1= 3).

YOUR MAGIC HOUR

To find the best hour in which to do
anything, simply add the month, day and
year of your birthday. Reduce it to a
single digit. The birth number tells you
the best hour to perform any undertaking,
A.M. or P.M.

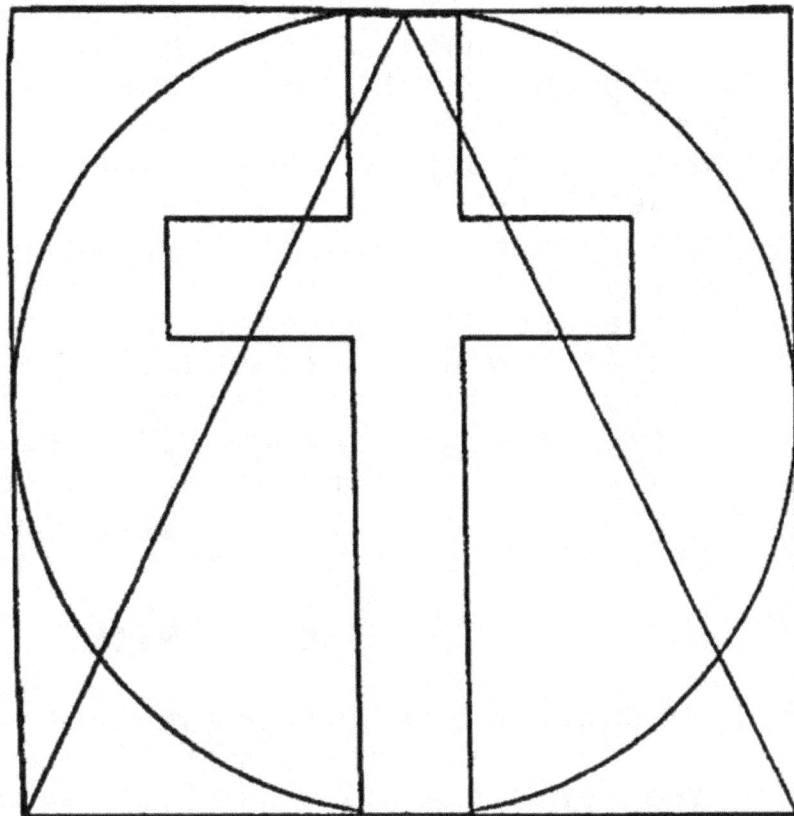

6.   SECRETS OF GOOD FORTUNE

In this chapter I will reveal many truths about money and good fortune. You can use these truths in your daily life for more prosperity and happiness. Do the practices carefully and faithfully and you will see the results. These practices can open up new opportunities to lead you into prosperous situations.

MONEY IS GOOD

The first thing you must do is erase any idea that money is evil. Many people like to quote from the Holy Bible, the scripture which says, "The love of money is the root of all evil." After hearing this scripture many times it becomes repetitive and therefore, creates a subconscious mental block against money. I will now explain to you what this scripture really means. The evilness of money would be to place more importance on money than on anything or anyone. Also, to love money to the point of craving or lusting after it, because one lacks it. This scripture does not mean that it is evil to have or want money.

LACK IS EVIL

To crave money because of the lack of it is the root of all evil. Many people are serving time in prison because of the lack of money. The person did not realize that their own self created limitation made it so. Therefore, they came to the conclusion that the only way to obtain

50

money was to be dishonest.

Many homes have been broken because a person became so obsessed with making money that they totally lost contact with their loved ones. Money is not evil of itself. Money is good and can assist you in the comfort and pleasures of life. Think how wonderful it would be to have enough money for everything you need and also be able to help others. Worry about money causes bad nerves and even physical illness. Money can bring peace of mind which then allows you to concentrate on important spiritual matters.

POWERFUL MONEY RITUALS

I will now share some of the universal prosperity laws with you. First I will give you the following exercises to remove any negative mental blocks you may have about money. Do them daily if it is possible

Exercise #1. Relax your physical body. Use the method I gave you on page 9 and 10 of this book. When you are relaxed, visualize yourself in a room of pure white. See a small green chest (like a jewelry box) on the floor. You may see this small chest as made of jade. On the top of this chest see the words "Money is good", in solid gold letters. Now open this chest and see money springing up out of it. It is like a fountain of water but it is money. Money of all denominations. It begins to cover the floor and pile up. Use your power of visualization to bring this money to you. After this exercise get up and forget about it until the next session.

Exercise #2. King David said in Psalms 23:1, "The Lord is my shepherd, I shall not want." A wonderful thing happens when we look to God for guidance. We, then, come to a state of living where we want for nothing but that which is good for us and those around us. With this in mind take a small piece of paper and write the following words. The Lord is my shepherd, I (insert your name here) shall not want. Place the paper where you will see it the first thing each morning and the last thing each night.

Be faithful in these practices and you will soon erase all mental blocks about money.

SEVEN MONEY SECRETS

God's greatest secret of good fortune is contained in the combined realization and principles set forth in the seven money secrets listed below.

MONEY SECRET #1 - Give freely to those in need. Do not wait until you are rich, give from what you have on hand.

MONEY SECRET #2 - Do not see what you give as coming from you. See it as coming from beyond you and flowing through you. There is an important reason for this. If you see what you give as coming from you there will arise a fear that you may deplete yourself. This is because most people think of self as being limited. When you see what you give as only flowing through you and coming from a higher, unlimited power, the fear has to leave.

MONEY SECRET #3 - When you give, do not

expect anything in return. Every good deed is an investment in the universal bank which comes back to you in time, many fold.

MONEY SECRET #4 - Quit thinking negative thoughts. Work on recreating your self image. See yourself as prospering in every way.

MONEY SECRET #5 - Quit speaking negative words. Let only positive words come from your lips. if you slip, correct yourself until positive speaking becomes a habit.

MONEY SECRET #6 - Spend money for what you like to do, with what you have to work with. This makes room for self satisfaction and for more riches to come into your life.

MONEY SECRET #7 - Observe the Golden Rule which says, "Do unto others what you would have them do unto you".

These principles are the universal laws which will help change your life and draw good fortune like a magnet. Remember this scripture, "Beloved, I wish above all things that you prosper......."The Third Epistle of John, Verse 2, (The Holy Bible).

7. THE SPOKEN WORD

Within the Holy Bible and other sacred writ are hidden words of power. These can be used as tools for manifesting certain accomplishments in your life. The Book of Psalms is one of the most popular and effective for this type of work.

Hidden in the Psalms are holy and powerful names of God and members of the Angelic Kingdom. In this chapter I will reveal the 22 words of power. These are within the 119th Psalm, which is the longest Psalm. However, for the most comprehensive study of all 150 Psalms, you should read my book, "Candle Burning Magic with the Psalms", published by Inner Light Publications. This book gives you a special formula on how to use the Divine Names of Power for each 150 Psalms.

The 22 words of power, as contained within the 119th. Psalm, concerns our present study. You should not repeat the name or the word of power out loud, only say it in your mind. Before using the divisions of the 119th. Psalm, observe the following 7 rules.

1. Light a white candle and burn some sandlewood incense. If it is possible, do not eat for a period of three hours prior to performing this exercise.

2. Enter a state of relaxation as you learned in Chapter one, page 9 and 10.

3. Try to improve your speaking habits. As you progress in this work you will develop a great power to create with your words. You do not want to create any negative conditions for yourself. Learn to speak positive about yourself, others and your situations in life.

4. Read the prescribed division of the Psalm aloud, from your heart with sincerity and emotion, followed by a prayer.

5. After reading the prescribed division of the Psalm and saying a prayer, mentally repeat the holy name of power. Do not say the holy name of power out loud.

6. While doing this part of your work, you must hold a mental picture of what you wish to accomplish.

7. After you finish your work, release it to the Higher power. The Higher power has a way of knowing just how to bring your desires into manifestation by Divine Wisdom.

22 WORDS OF POWER

You will notice that the 119th. Psalm is divided into 22 sections of 8 verses. At the head of each division is a single word. These are words of personal power and the fact of 8 verses to each division has great significance; 8 is the number of a new beginning. The word at the head of each division is one of the letters of the Hebrew Alphabet. They have been called the Alphabet of the Magi. This is because each of these words are very powerful and have a special significance.

They can lead the wise student to realms of cosmic consciousness. Following is the list of the 22 divisions with their uses according to the ancient tradition.

PSALM 119
ALEPH

VERSES 1-8 It is said that those who speak these verses in a solemn and even tone of voice can stop quivering of the limbs. Also, one will find the means to fulfill promises.

PSALM 119
BETH

VERSES 9-16 You can obtain a good memory by reading these verses on Thursday night after fasting all day.

PSALM 119
GIMEL

VERSES 17-24 It is believed these verses relieve eye pain. To be said seven times in succession.

PSALM 119
DALETH

VERSES 25-32 To be said eight times in succession every day when involved in a lawsuit. When you seek advise repeat the verses ten times.

PSALM 119
HE

VERSES 33-40 To repeat these verses will keep you from committing sins.

PSALM 119
VAU

VERSES 41-48 Speak over a glass of water for your child. It is said that the child will become obedient and will not give you problems.

PSALM 119
ZAIN

VERSES 49-56 If you have been led cunningly into a hurtful situation by a evil person/persons, repeat this eighteen times. You may then withdraw without injury to yourself.

PSALM 119
CHETH

VERSES 57-64 It is said to bring healing of pains in the upper parts of the body when repeated over wine and given to drink.

PSALM 119
TETH

VERSES 65-72 It is believed to heal pains in the kidneys when repeated reverently over the sick person.

PSALM 119
JOD

VERSES 73-80 Say this at the end of your morning prayer and your prayers will be heard and answered.

PSALM 119
CAPH

VERSES 81-88 Pray and say ten times in a

low voice to relieve sores on the right
side of the nose.

PSALM 119
LAMED

VERSES 89-96   Read these verses after
your evening prayer when you must appear
before a judge the following day.

PSALM 119
MEM

VERSES 97-104   It is said that to pray
these seven times for three days, will
relieve pain in the right limbs or hands.

PSALM 119
NUN

VERSES 105-112 Said to grant you a safe
and happy journey.

PSALM 119
SAMECH

VERSES 113-120 Pray these before you ask
a favor of a superior.

PSALM 119
AIN

VERSES 121-128 It is said to pray these
seven times for three days, will relieve
pain in the left limbs or hands.

PSALM 119
PE

VERSES 129-136 It is said this cures
swelling on the left side of the nose.

PSALM 119
TSADDI

VERSES 137-144 Pray these three times before a decision.

PSALM 119
KOPH

VERSES 145-152 It is believed that this cures pains in the left leg by saying over rose oil and then anointing the leg with this oil

PSALM 119
RESH

VERSES 153-160 It is believed to cure a running boil in the right ear.

PSALM 119
SCHIN

VERSES 161-168 It is said that to say these words three times over olive oil in a low prayerful voice, will relieve severe headaches when applied.

PSALM 119
TAU

VERSES 169-176 Said to relieve boil in the left ear.

In employing the 22 words of personal power, remember always that you are working with something sacred. Do not reveal to every one what you are doing. You may use this knowledge to help yourself and others, but always have any physical symptoms checked by a doctor before and after any devotional applications.

8. TRUE PSYCHIC POWERS

The word psychic means a person who is sensitive and aware of things and people without depending upon the physical senses. Mystics of all ages have taught that man possesses a sixth and seventh sense beyond the five physical senses.

All people have psychic faculties but they are undeveloped in the average person. By means of special exercises and mind expanding methods one can develop these psychic abilities.

A psychic may or may not be a spiritual person. Some groups who lack spirituality are conducting research into psychic phenomena. A spiritual person can use psychic abilities with the help of spiritual entities, depending upon the person's development.

In this chapter I explain the various psychic powers, the methods for their use and how to develop these powers.

CORRECT DEVELOPMENT

Before you do any of the practices to develop your psychic powers you should follow these guide lines. It is important to realize that these powers must be devoloped correctly and along certain lines of positive spirituality. I do not recommend anyone to take this study lightly. The horrible examples of incorrect development haunt us throughout history. Institutions for the insane are

filled with people who hear voices and
see into other dimensions. Psychopathic
killers claim that voices, or God's voice
told them to murder their victims. A
person who plays with psychic power can
fall prey to negative entities and evil
spirits who wish to possess and destroy.
Develop your powers by using the
techniques I discussed in chapter 1 and
then protect yourself by using the
methods I taught in chapter 2. Only then
should you try to develop your psychic
power.

When you feel safe in the knowledge
that you have elevated yourself into a
state of positive consciousness, only
good things will be attracted to you from
the higher levels of life. Consider the
words of Master Jesus which are
appropriate on this subject:
" And I say unto you, ask, and it shall
be given you: Seek, and ye shall find:
Knock and it shall be open. If a son
shall ask bread of any of you that is a
father, will he give him a stone? Or if
he ask a fish, will he for a fish give
him a serpent? Or if he shall ask for an
egg, will he offer him a scorpion? If ye
then, being evil, know how to give good
gifts unto your children: How much more
shall your Heavenly Father give the Holy
Spirit to them that ask Him."
St. Luke 11:9-13

THE GREAT MAGIC WORD

ABRACADABRA - This word was originally
used by the Magi to expedite development
into higher planes of consciousness. It
was worn as an amulet, engraved or
written in the form of a triangle by the
Holy Magi. Its numerical values are 22

for the path which attains to the Tree of
Life; Number 12, which means governmental
perfection, relating to the development
of character in harmony with the Twelve
Tribes of Israel, the Twelve Apostles of
Jesus and the Twelve Gates of the New
Jerusalem. Number 3 which is symbolic of
the Holy Trinity. It is written as shown
below.

```
            A
           A B
          A B R
         A B R A
        A B R A C
       A B R A C A
      A B R A C A D
     A B R A C A D A
    A B R A C A D A B
   A B R A C A D A B R
  A B R A C A D A B R A
```

To develop psychic abilities do the
following. You may copy this magical word
on a small piece of white paper. Some
people prefer to use parchment, a quill
pen and Dove's Blood Brand Ink. This is
available through occult shops, locally
or through the mail. After you have
copied the word you should place it under
a crystal ball. If you do not have a
crystal ball you may use a clear glass
bowl filled with water. Place a black
cloth on a table. Place the magical word
under your crystal ball or glass bowl.
Light a candle and place it to your left.
Gaze at the magical word under the bowl
or crystal ball. Do this for as long a
time as you feel comfortable.

PSYCHIC SIGHT

CLAIRVOYANCE - This means "clear-seeing",

and manifests in two ways: The first is to see things, around yourself or another person, that others cannot see. It may appear that you see invisible entitles, auras, other dimensions, etc., with your physical eyes. But, actually, you are seeing these things with your "third eye" or intuitive sixth sense. The second way that this ability manifests is to know, sense or perceive by intuition, that an invisible someone or array of impressions are coming into your range of clairvoyant ability. Most psychics use this second type of clairvoyance; when they say that they see something about the person, what most of them really mean is that they sense it at an intuitive level.

HOW TO DEVELOP CLAIRVOYANCE

Light a candle, set it on a table, turn all other lights off and seat yourself in front of the candle. Just gaze at the candle for several moments. Mentally desire to see the magnetic field around the candle flame. Continue wanting to see the finer vibrations of color and symbolic images around the flame, while doing this also think of the spot between your eyebrows. This shifting of your consciousness back and forth, between wanting to see the magnetic field of the flame and thinking of the spot between your eyebrows, will help you to see with clairvoyant vision. Anytime you wish to see the colorful magnetic field around a person, do this practice. Continue this practice once or twice weekly until, and after you get results.

PSYCHIC HEARING

CLAIRAUDIENCE - This word means "clear
63

hearing", and also manifests in two ways:
The first is where the mystic seems to
actually be hearing words from an
invisible person, or a conversation
taking place in another dimension. They
may also hear words that were spoken by
or to the person for whom they are giving
a reading. Actually, they are not hearing
with the physical sense of hearing; they
only seem to hear in that way. It is also
with their sixth sense that they are able
to hear. The second way that one
experiences clairaudience ability is when
the words come to them in "a strong
thought". In other words, the message
makes itself known in a series of words,
seeming to saturate our consciousness.
When this happens, we know somehow that
it is not our thoughts, but a message
from the invisible realms.

HOW TO DEVELOP CAIRAUDIENCE

Sit quietly in a room with soft lights.
Relax your physical body as taught to you
in chapter 1. The room should be very
quiet, at an hour when there will be a
minimum of outside noises. Sit for
several moments listening to the silence.
After awhile, direct your thinking
inwardly to the sound of silence and
peace. In a short time you may begin to
hear what sounds like music or bells.
Keep thinking upon these sounds, desiring
that you receive a message. When your
session is complete, write down any
impressions you received. In the future,
you may tune in to the inner sound while
in another person's presence, to see what
you can pick up in their behalf. Do this
private exercise once or twice weekly.

BIBLICAL EXAMPLES OF
THE POWERS OF CLAIRAUDIENCE / CLAIRVOYANCE

"And he fell to the earth, and heard a voice.....And the men which journeyed with him stood speechless, hearing a voice, but seeing no man"... Acts 9:4-7

"And, behold, there appeared unto them Moses and Elias talking with him"...
Matthew 17:3

"Before Phillip called thee, when thou wast under the fig tree, I saw thee"..
John 1:48

"And there came an Angel of the Lord... And the angel appeared to him and said.."
Judges 6:11-12

PSYCHIC FEELING

PSYCHOMETRY-This means "clear-feeling". In this ability, the mystic holds an object in their left hand, and picks up vibrations about the owner of the object. This is possible because we leave a magnetic record of our feelings, thoughts and personality on anything we use or own.

HOW TO DEVELOP PSYCHOMETRY

Ask the assistance of a friend for practicing this ability. Have them give you an object to hold in your left hand. They should be familiar with some of the history of the object, but it should be something of which you know nothing about. As you hold the object, relax in the manner already taught to you. Then mentally ask to know something about the object's past, as well as its owner. As you receive intuitive impressions, relate them to the person. Do not stop and ask if you are correct. Let the information flow until you know that you are finished.

Another method to develop psychometry is to have someone place a few pieces of spice or dry food in an envelope without your knowledge of what it is. Hold the envelope and desire to actually taste or smell what is in it. The first mental impression is usually the correct one. Remember, practice makes perfect. Do not be discouraged if you do not always obtain accurate results.

You may also practice your ability when you receive mail. Hold the letter in your hand for a few moments to see if you can pick up an indication of what's written in the letter.

MEDIUMSHIP

Spirit Communication- This is the ability of establishing a link of communication between the spirits of the departed and the living.

There seems to be conviction among most modern day christians that it is wrong to communicate with the dead. However, there is a great misunderstanding of terms in regards to this subject.

BIBLICAL PROOF OF SPIRIT COMMUNICATION

The conviction of the dogmatists seem to be founded upon a scripture found in the Old Testament of the Holy Bible. It

66

is, "Why, consult the dead on behalf of the living?", Isaiah 8:19. I will now attempt to explain. To most people the word "dead" means one of two things, depending upon their religious belief. The first is that it means, the ceasing of life, totally and finally. The second is that it means the spirit of man being separated from the body. In the spiritual sense the word "dead" means more. The Holy Scriptures refer to the word "dead" as the unregenerated, or sinners. Study the following scriptures.

"And you hath He quickened, who were dead in trespasses and sins".. Ephesians 2:1

"Even when we were dead in sins"......... Ephesians 2:5

"And you, being dead in your sins"....... Colossians 2:13

"But she that liveth in pleasure is dead while she yet liveth"... I Timothy 5:6

"And another of his disciples said unto him, Lord, suffer me first to go and bury my father. But Jesus said unto him, follow me; and let the dead bury their dead"...... St. Matthew 8:21-22

We see by these scriptures that they who were unregenerated, or walking in spiritual darkness, were considered dead even though they were physically alive. Therefore, it is not wrong to communicate with spirits. It is just wrong if you attempt to communicate with spirits of a low order of consciousness or the spiritually dead. This is because low order spirits will lead you away from the path of the true and living God. They want you to join them in their sufferings of walking in a state of Hell. They seek to confuse, trick, possess, and destroy. This is why it is so important to raise your consciousness into higher planes and be well protected before attempting contact with the spirits. You will then know the differences between the grades and motives of spirits who attempt to communicate with you. Remember the following scripture.

"Beloved, believe not every spirit, but try the spirits whether they are of God: Because many false prophets, (False Mediums), are gone out into the world..."

I John 4:1

THREE TYPES OF MEDIUMS

A medium is a person who is a channel for spirit entities to communicate with the physically alive. The three types of mediums are:

1. **Mental Mediums**-This is a person who receives mental impressions and messages from Spirits, Master Teachers and Angels. They communicate this information to their clients.

2. **Trance Mediums**-This is a person who goes into a trance so that the spirits speak through them.

3. **Manifestation Mediums**-This is one who is able to cause physical manifestations to prove the presence of the spirit, even producing a materialization of the spirit.

68

A person may possess one, two or all three of the mediumistic abilities to a certain degree.

BIBLICAL EXAMPLES OF MEDIUMSHIP

Mediumship is recorded in the Holy Bible as being demonstrated by various prophets. The word Prophet may be considered synonymous with the word Medium.

Spirit Writing-This is an ability in which someone may write a message or even a book, under the control of a spirit. King David gave his son, Solomon, a diagram from which to build the Lord's Temple. He said it came to him in writing as the hand of the Lord was upon him.
I Chronicles 28:19

The Trance-The trance state has many scriptural examples. They are:

"He hath said, which heard the words of God, which saw the vision of the Almighty, falling into a trance......"
Numbers 24:4

"....Peter went upon the housetop to pray ....He fell into a trance and saw Heaven opened....." Acts 10:9-11

"And it came to pass, that, even while I prayed in the temple, I was in a trance.."
Acts 22:17

"And I knew such a man, whether in the body, or out of the body, I cannot tell: God knoweth; how that he was caught up into paradise, and heard unspeakable words...." II Corinthians 12:3,4

Materialization-- Apportation is our next mediumistic ability under consideration. An apport is an object, animal, or human which has been dematerialized from one location (so as to give the appearance of vanishing), and the elements rematerialized in another location as if to appear out of thin air. This is accomplished by the applied will power of a living Magi or by a person with the aid of a powerful spirit. See the following Biblical example;

"..And when they were come up out of the water, the Spirit of the Lord caught away Philip, and the Eunuch saw him no more.. but Philip was found at Azotus."

Acts 8:39,40

Levitation-At times an apport is not dematerialized but rises and floats to another location. This falls under the classification of levitation. Many Yogis, as well as Western Mystics were said to rise above the ground while sitting, standing or walking in a state of great spiritual devotion. It is recorded that Jesus walked on water.

"And when they saw him walking upon the sea, they supposed it had been a spirit.. ..."

St. Mark 6:49

"But as one was felling a beam, the ax head fell into the water: And he cried, and said, Alas, Master! For it was borrowed. And the man of God said, Where fell it? And he shewed him the place. And He (the man of God) cut down a stick, and

70

cast it thither; and the iron did swim.."
                                    II Kings 6:5,6

"Jesus said, "The works that I do shall
he (who believes in me) do also."
                                    St. John 14:12

Inspired Speaking- Speaking in a
foreign language: A person may, under the
influence of Holy Spirit Guides, speak in
a language that they have not learned
consciously. This would be for the
benefit of the hearer who did understand
the language, and show proof of a genuine
spirit manifestation.

Speaking unknown languages is another
mediumistic ability, also called
"Speaking in Unknown Tongues". The
scriptural examples are found in Acts,
Chapter 2 and also in I Corinthians
14:27-32.

HOW TO DEVELOP MEDIUMSHIP

First, and MOST IMPORTANT, use the
protection techniques I gave in chapter
2, before any attempt to make contact
with the Spirit World. The reason for
this, is that there are many spirits who
are earthbound, and love to play tricks
on people. You must be sure that you are
communicating with highly evolved
spirits, who would not ask you to do
anything against your highest good, or
that of others. The Holy Spirits always
advise one to participate in wholesome
things that will benefit humankind,
beginning with the medium and anyone
depending upon them.

TELEPATHY

Thought transference or mental telepathy has been a subject of psychic development for many generations. The idea is that two persons may communicate mentally within the same room or at a distance. It also means that one may send a thought to another. It is important to realize that for a person to receive a thought sent by another, it is necessary for the receiver to be in a passive state of mind. To send a thought, form a mental picture of the person you wish to contact. Before you do this, however, it is best to go into a state of relaxation. After you visualize the person, tell them your message, mentally or out loud. Then forget it until the next time. You may have to try more than once; remember, they must be in a passive state of mind to receive your message.

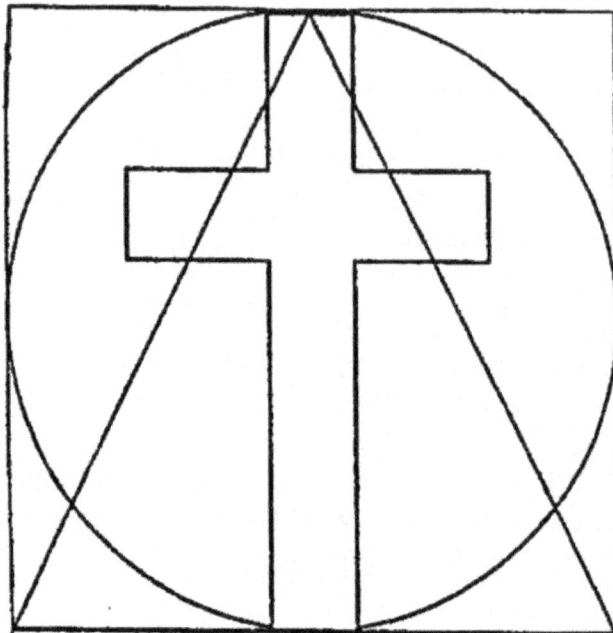

9.   MAKE A MAGIC MIRROR

In this chapter I will share some valuable information concerning the mystic use of mirrors. You may use any mirror if it is prepared according to my instructions. You will need, as part of your preparation, the following items; blessed olive oil, a white candle, and a bowl in which you will place consecrated water. Bless the oil by the instructions on page 41. Prepare the white candle to attract, by the instructions on page 43.

WHY USE A MIRROR?

THE PURPOSE-You may accomplish the following things by using the magic mirror: Influence yourself to change habits; Communicate with the subconscious and superconscious minds; Develop spiritual sight; Ask questions of higher intelligence; Meditate; See past lives and much more.

WHEN TO USE A MIRROR

The Time-The best time of the month to do this is the first seven days before the full moon. Do not use the mirror during the full moon, only during the seven days before the full moon. Check your calendar or almanac for this schedule of the moon. The best time of the day to do this is at night between the hours of twelve midnight and four A.M. The vibrations of the earth are of a certain stillness during these hours. The solitude will help you be more receptive to spiritual impressions. You should be quiet and alone so you will not be distracted.

THE FIRST STEP

The Preparation-Boil Some water. After it has started to boil repeat the Twenty Third Psalm from the Holy Bible over the water. Allow the water to cool. Using a clean cloth or paper towel, apply the water to the mirror, covering all areas of the mirror with it.

After the water has dried on the mirror, take some blessed olive oil on the first or second finger of your right hand.Apply the oil on the center of the mirror, then smear it from the center in a line straight down, then from the center straight up. You will then smear it from the center in a line to your left and finally from the center in a line to your right. This forms a cross. See diagram below.

Allow this to dry. Then wash the mirror with soap and water. This preparation should be done when you are alone during the hours already mentioned and during the seven days before the full moon. You should save the water in a jar, as this is consecrated water and will be used in the work of this lesson.

THE SECOND STEP

The final preparation-When you are ready for your work, do the following things. First, draw the diagram below on your mirror. You can use a felt tip marker, as this should wipe off easily. Mark the G in the upper left hand corner.

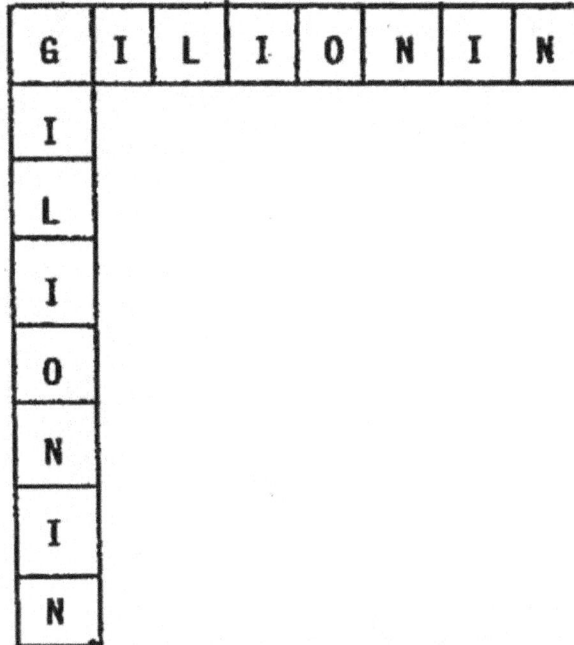

G	I	L	I	O	N	I	N
I
L
I
O
N
I
N

After you draw the squares and letters on the mirror, place a bowl of the consecrated water between where you will sit and the mirror. Place the candle to your right.

THE THIRD STEP

When you have made all preparations and are ready to begin, bathe yourself and relax mentally by meditation on the positive results you wish to obtain. Try to keep yourself from getting upset during the day of your work.

THE RITUAL

Now you are ready to begin. First, light the candle. Then repeat the Lord's Prayer. Be sure all lights are out except the light of the candle. Gaze into the mirror looking into the eyes of your reflected image. After several minutes, speak out loud in a soft but firm voice, your reason for doing this work. For example, if you wish to change unwanted habits, you must clearly state that which you wish to stop doing and that which you desire to replace it. A very good way to change is to address your subconscious mind, asking it to reject the unwanted trait from now on and to accept that which is constructive and good. You would then request that your superconscious mind guide you into the help that you need. It is very wise and knows how to help you.

You may ask questions of higher intelligence, such as Master Teachers, Angels, Saints and Spirit Guides. It may be that you will see a vision as you gaze into the mirror or the answer may come to you in a flash of intuition. The answer may come as a dream later that night. Do not try to predetermine how the answer will come. Be open to the best way for you to receive the answer according to God's wisdom.

Gazing at your image and visualizing rays of light coming from the eyes and going into the eyes of your image, will develop a keener spiritual sight.

TAKING CARE OF YOUR MIRROR

If you wish, you can buy a mirror just for this purpose so you do not have to prepare it every time. In this case you can paint the diagram on it instead of using the felt pen. However, you must keep it wrapped in a violet colored cloth when not in use. It would be good to wash it with the consecrated water and apply the oil, as the instructions I have already given you, every ninety days.

After each session throw the water in the bowl away. Also, keep a pad and pen next to your bed so that you may write down any dreams or experience you have during the night. Much information is lost because we fail to write it down during the moment that we awake. If we go back to sleep and wake up later, we will forget much. Be consistent in your work and you will be rewarded from the higher planes of being.

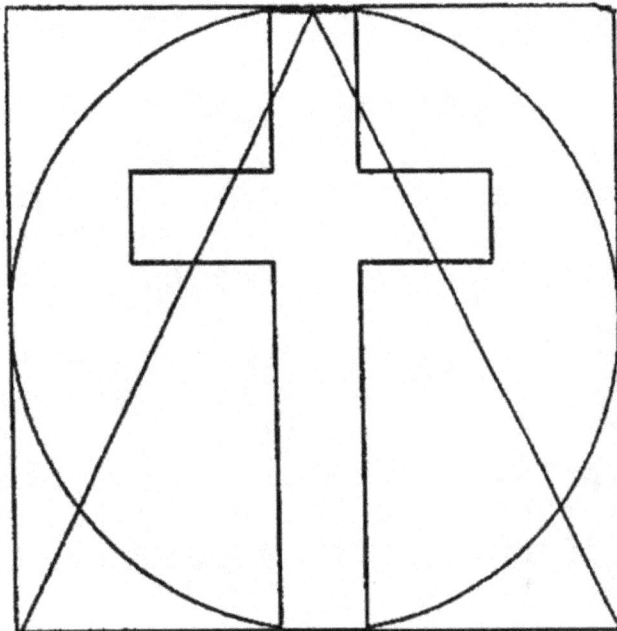

10. TALISMANIC MAGIC

Mystic Seals are legendary talismans, said to contain special vibrations for specific purposes. It is believed that certain words and designs have virtues sealed within them. According to the Inner Teachings, powerful spirits revealed the designs of certain seals to the Magi, Prophets and Adepts.

Some of the legendary seals contain hidden names of the God-Power. Others contain the names of angels or specific forces of nature.

The designs on mystic seals can awaken special powers within the human mind, so that the practitioner can release the energy to the Higher Power. The Higher Power receives this energy and sends it back into our world in the form of favorable circumstances that enhance success.

In addition to the revelation given to the Wise Ones about these things, there is the great power of belief from the minds of multiplied thousands of people, who have used these seals for ages.

Talismanic Magic is one of the easiest forms of Inner Pathworking, because it is a quiet practice. One may not have the privacy for elaborate candleburning, or other rituals, but working with talismans affords you a private means of magical work.

FIVE POWERFUL TALISMANS
OF THE SACRED MAGIC

The talismans in this book may be cut out and used as instructed, however, you may wish to order a set separately. You can receive a set by writing to the publisher, Inner Light Publications, and requesting information about them.

The first four talismans are said to originate with King Solomon. The fifth is a miniature replica of the Staff of Moses. Cut out each talisman and hold them between the palms of your hand, one at a time. While you are holding the talisman in your hand say the following words:
"Blessed Be; may the Cosmic unity blend with my High Self and bring forth all my desires through this symbol of power. So mote it be."

. Following is a list of the enclosed talismans with their alleged mystic virtues. You may choose to seal your talismans in plastic to preserve them.

#1 The Seal of Protection

CUT OUT THE TALISMAN ON THE OTHER SIDE OF THIS PAGE.

#1 The Seal of Protection

The Seal of Protection talisman is to be worn on the left side of the body.

#1 PROTECTION
Write your name here

#2 The Seal of Magnetic Power

The Seal of Magnetic Power is believed
to help one to become stronger and more
magical. It is to be worn on the right
side of the body.

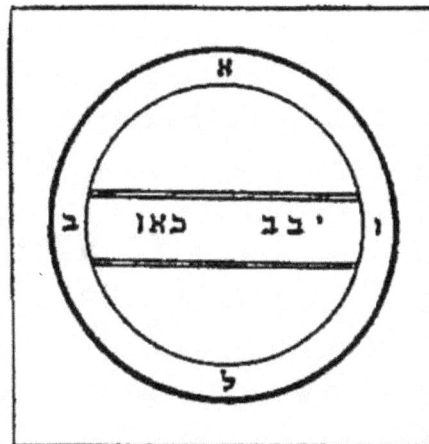

#3 The Wishing Seal

The Wishing Seal is to be placed
between your palms when you are praying
for a wish to be granted. It is believed
that all wishes, not in violation of
cosmic law, will be granted.

CUT OUT THE TALISMANS ON THE OTHER SIDE
OF THIS PAGE.

#2 MAGNETISM
Write Your Name Here

#3 WISHING
Write Your Name Here

#4 The Seal of Rest

The Seal of Rest. It is said that this sacred talisman should be kept under your pillow for a restful sleep and to help obtain more significant dreams.

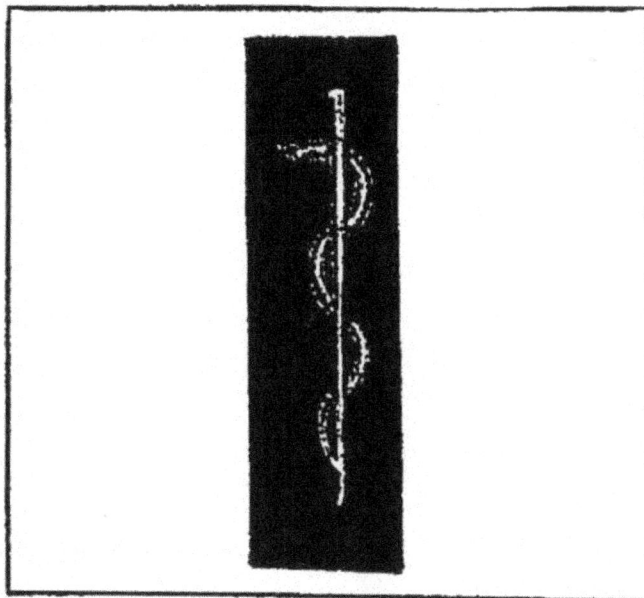

#5 The Seal of the Staff of Moses

The Staff of Moses Seal is to be held in your right hand when doing any work described in this book.

CUT OUT THE TALISMANS ON THE OTHER SIDE
OF THIS PAGE.

#4 RESTFUL SLEEP
Write Your Name Here

#5 STAFF OF MOSES
Write Your Name Here

THE HAND OF GLORY

This is the complete illustrated version of the famous Hand of Glory. It is also called Hand of the Mysteries. For many centuries mystics believed that to have even a picture of this powerful symbol in their home would protect their dwelling from all evil works, of any secret enemy or spirit who would come into the their home. However, there was a secret ritual which activated the power of the hand. I now share that ritual with you. Keep the following instructions secret - they are for you and you alone.

During the seventh day before the Full Moon you are to take a handful of salt in your right hand. Hold it tightly so that your vibrations will impregnate the salt. As you do this, repeat the 91st. Psalm. After each verse you direct your eyes away from the Bible and look at the picture for a few moments. Then continue by reading the next verse until you have read all sixteen verses and directed your gaze to the hand sixteen times. Then you are to sprinkle the salt all over the picture. After you do this set a candle holder containing a white or purple candle which you have blessed to attract, (See page 43). Place the candle on the center of the picture and burn it for a few moments each night until the first night of the Full Moon. The next and final step is to hide the picture in your home. You may place it on a table under a covering, or place it behind another picture in a frame. See page 89.

The symbolism in the picture is very

85

significant: At the bottom right is a
sunrise, this is symbolic of our efforts
or action coming forth from the right
side. At the bottom left is the moon and
star against the evening sky. This is
symbolic of our passive state on the left
side from which we receive vibrations. In
the center of the hand is The Pentagram
or Magical Star with a Cross at its core.
This means that we are to develop The
Sacred Magical Power along lines of pure
spirituality. Above the five fingers are
the following symbols: The Crown with a
Cross, which means reward through work
and perseverance. The Six-Pointed Star,
symbolic of blending human will with
Divine Will. The flame, which stands for
the zeal and force of The Holy Spirit.
The Fish, that tells us that we are to
search for the Inner Self. And The Key,
which reveals the clue to understanding
the mysteries are in small things. It
also represents The Master Key to all
things.

There are four elements of the physical
world, and a fifth element of higher
energy. We will not go into an expanded
study of the elements but you should know
the relationship between the five fingers
and the five elements. I will also give
you the explanation of how these elements
relate to our feelings and desires.

The thumb relates to the element of
earth and corresponds to material matters
and grounding. The first finger relates
to the element of air and corresponds to
mental matters. The second finger relates
to the element of fire and corresponds to
emotional matters. The third finger
relates to the element of water and is in
correspondence with higher expression of

thought and emotions. The little finger relates to the fifth element of Spirit. Spirit is present in all space and time, for without it, nothing else could exist. The correspondence for Spirit is the inspiration of the Highest Order. This is The Master Key to self and Divine realization.

After following all instructions for consecrating the Hand of Glory, dispose of anything left of the candle and salt. You may do this in any way that you see fit. Some people choose to dispose of the items by burying them. Others dispose of the items by putting them in the trash. In any case these items have served their purpose, and therefore it is up to you.

Following are some Biblical examples of the power of the hand, human and Divine.

"I (the Divine Spirit) will cover thee with my hand..........."
Exodus 33:22

"And Jonathan ...... strengthened his hand in God (The Divine Power)".
I Samuel 23:16

"......there arises a little cloud (vision) out of the sea, like a man's hand......."
I Kings 18:44

"He that has clean hands, can reach the mountain (The High Order Of Divine Realization) ....."
Psalm 24:4

William Oribello burns candles for good luck, to celebrate release of revised edition of *Sacred Magic.*

THE HAND OF GLORY

PS.91

**CUT OUT THE TALISMAN ON THE OTHER SIDE
OF THIS PAGE.**

Write Your Name Here

11. CHANGE YOUR LIFE NOW

In closing, I will share several practices which you may perform daily. One of the most important things to remember is this: ALWAYS PERFORM THE RELAXATION TECHNIQUE GIVEN IN CHAPTER ONE, BEFORE PERFORMING ANY OF THE FOLLOWING EXERCISES, AS THIS WILL BRING THE BEST RESULTS.

THE DAILY PRAYER

Shortly after waking up, the following prayer should be repeated softly, but with feeling and sincerity;

"Universal Mind, fill my day with Divine Cosmic Love and Harmony. Give me the guidance, courage and wisdom to face and successfully deal with the events of this day, for the highest good of myself and all others whose lives touch mine. Protect me from all danger, seen and unseen. Thank you. It is done."

NIGHTLY PRAYER

Before going to sleep, repeat the following prayer (you may say this mentally if you wish):

"Universal Mind, protect, teach and heal me as I sleep. If I have violated any universal laws this day, either by commission or omission, please forgive me. Thank you. It is done."

MAGNETIC BREATHING

This exercise is, for all practical purposes, your "Daily Bread" to empower every level of your being. It is a way of accumulating and storing what was termed "The Secret Force" and "Magnetism" by my early teachers. This force is the very essence of Universal Life and has been known by other terms, Such as "Prana", "Odic Force", "Vital Life Force", and ect. It does not matter which term is used, the Force is one.

You can use this Force as a conductor for healing, the will to break bad habits, have more magnetism in your personality, and to generally charge all your magical operations with more power. I will give you two versions of this exercise: The first is simple and quick. The second is more involved and takes more time, but you should avail yourself of the second version whenever you possibly can.

THE FIRST VERSION

The first version of the magnetic breath is as follows: Sit or stand facing the East. Take several deep breaths, and as you do so, imagine that an egg-shaped cloud of white mist has gathered around you. Now inhale deeply, only this time, imagine that you are inhaling this mist through every pore of your skin, all over your physical body. Will that this energy be stored with your physical, emotional, and mental levels of your being. Because you have, by your God Given ability of creative imagination,

92

attracted such a Force, your spiritual self will also be enhanced.

Continue taking this Cosmic Energy into you each time you inhale; each time you exhale, imagine that you are letting go of all things that hinder you, releasing them into the transforming power of God's Light. Do this practice for as long or short of a time as you desire. Be sure to take all of the mist that you mentally attracted into your being.

THE SECOND VERSION

The second version of the magnetic breath requires that you stand, face the east and stretch out your arms from side to side, forming a human cross image. Now as you inhale deeply, imagine that you are drawing the power of the air element into your being, through the pores of your skin. As you exhale, you are letting go of all things that hinder you.

Now turn to the south, with your arms still outstretched. Inhale while you imagine that you are drawing the power of the fire element into your being, through the pores of your skin. As you exhale, you are letting go of all things that hinder you.

Now turn to the west, with your arms still outstretched. Inhale while you imagine that you are drawing the power of the water element into your being, through the pores of your skin. As you exhale, you are letting go of all things that hinder you.

Finally, turn to the north, with your arms still outstretched. Inhale while you
93

imagine that you are drawing the power of the earth element into your being, through the pores of your skin. As you exhale, you are letting go of all things that hinder you.

In closing this second version of the Magnetic Breath, turn back to the east. Inhale deeply and exhale strongly, positioning your lips as though you are whistling, making a sound like a strong wind blowing through the trees.

MASTERY OF THOUGHT

By thinking, we create our everyday realities as well as our destinies. It is imperative that you become a "watcher", to guard against the negative thoughts that cross your mind.

Each time a negative thought comes into you mind, see a fire arise and burn up the negative thought. Then, instantly replace it with a positive thought, totally opposite of the negative. In doing this you will be able to discipline your mind.

MASTERY OF THE SPOKEN WORD

"In the beginning was the word....And the word was God"
St. John 1:1

As one advances in any type of magical training, they will realize that they are becoming a god, able to speak things into existence by the force of their will power. Therefore, it is important that if we say anything negative about ourselves, other people and objects, that we instantly contradict ourselves out loud

94

by saying the opposite. In Italian Mystical Folklore, people use the term "God Forbid" when they speak of anything negative that could happen.

THERE'S MORE

If you decide to go no further than this book, then you possess a valuable tool, which if applied properly, can set you on the path towards finding a true teacher. Remember the ancient axiom: "When the pupil is ready, the teacher appears." However, if you feel guided to write me for information regarding further training, you may do so at the address below.

And now, dear friend, may the Eternal Light of Universal Mind guide you in the right direction, and crown all of your efforts with abundant success.

William Alexander Oribello
c/o INNER LIGHT PUBLICATIONS
P.O. BOX 753
NEW BRUNSWICK, N.J. 08903

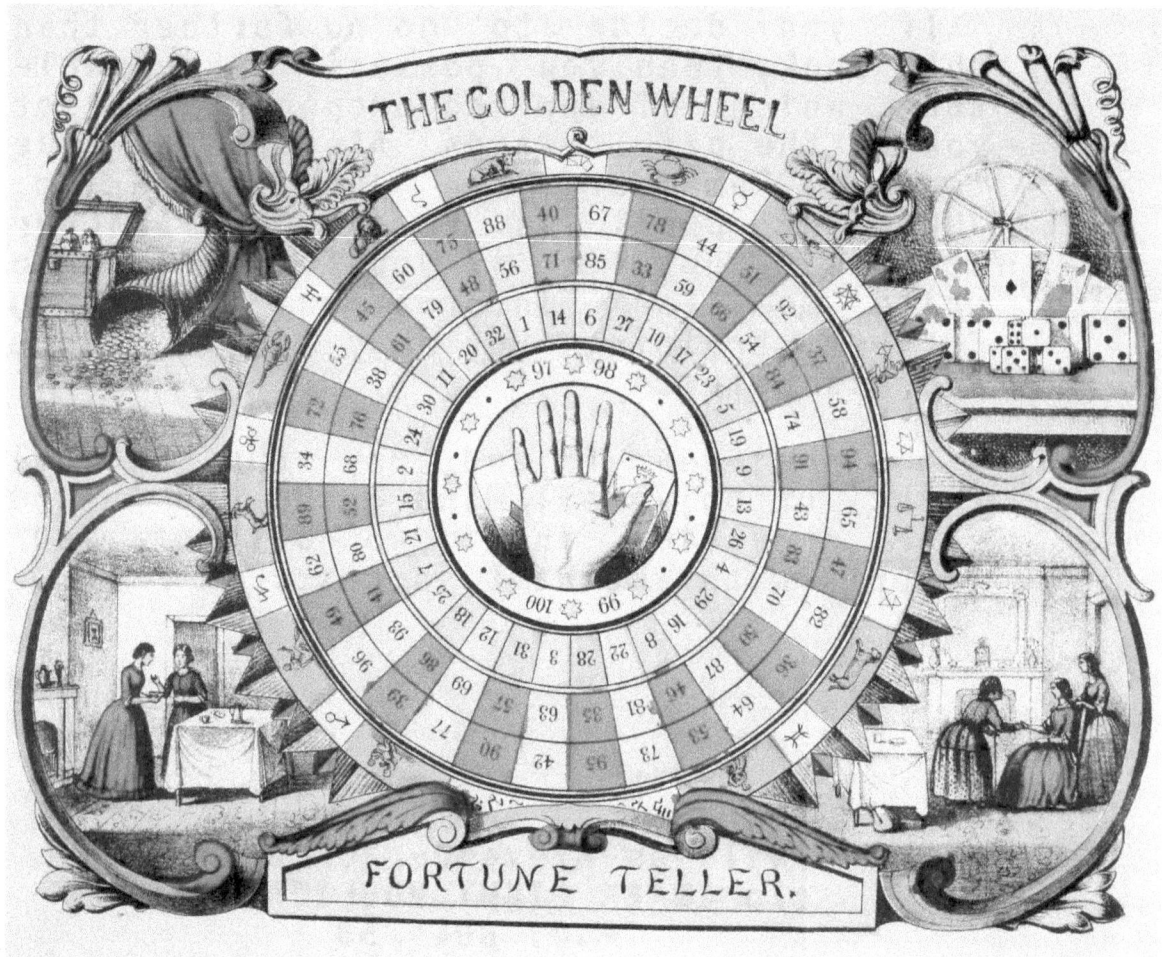

Make A Copy Of This Image To Tell Your Fortune.

THE GOLDEN WHEEL OF FORTUNE

This singular wheel was much consulted in the middle ages, and is said to have been used by Cagliostro to aid him in his divination I have selected it from an old Latin manuscript on Astrology, and translated it into English for the benefit of those of my readers who cannot read the former language.

THE GOLDEN WHEEL OF FORTUNE SHOWS: **I.** Whether you shall obtain the favor of the person you desire? **II.** Will your wishes come true or not? **III.** How long it will take a sick person recover. **IV.** Shall your expectation or wish succeed? **V.** If it is good for you to marry, or otherwise? **VI.** Whether the friendship of a certain person will prove advantageous or not. **VII.** Whether a person shall be rich or poor? etc.

HOW TO TELL FORTUNES BY THE GOLDEN WHEEL

The guidelines are very simple. It is a matter of closing ones eyes and letting your finger or pointer fall upon the Golden Wheel of Fortune. Do not over think this amazing oracle. For it is often the simplest things in life that carry the most meaning.

The person whose fortune is to be told, must place the Golden Wheel of Fortune on a flat surface in front of them. They then must close their eyes and think about what they want. They must try to visualize in their mind what it is that they seek. Keeping their eyes closed, and using their finger or a pencil, lower it onto the surface of the Golden Wheel. If done correctly, ones finger or pointer should be on a number. Now refer in the next section for an explanation, which stands at the corresponding number that is indicated.

Remember that the first answer is usually the correct one. Repeating the question in hopes of obtaining a more satisfactory answer will only lead to misinterpretations and error. If the answer given is not satisfactory, think about what you can change in your life to make your desire a reality. Afterwards, wait seven days before asking again.

The following observations answer for either sex, the party, therefore, trying this wheel, must alter wife for husband, or just as the answer may suit either party.

THE GOLDEN WHEEL OF FORTUNE
ANSWERS

1. If this number is fixed upon, it assures the person that they will marry will be successful, but not necessarily the best looking.

2. Whatever your intentions are, for the present, decline them. Those absent will return.

3. Shows loss of friends; bad success at law; loss of money; unfaithfulness in love.

4. If your desires are extravagant, they will not be granted; but mind how you make use of your fortune.

5. Very good fortune; sudden prosperity; great respect from high personages; a letter bringing important news.

6. Look well to those who owe you money. You may get a text or email from them soon.

7. Your lover will act constant and true toward you.

8. A friend will be very successful soon, by which you will be much benefited.

9. A loving partner; success in your undertakings; a healthy life and family.

10. Your husband will not have a great fortune, but with your assistance the two of you can live a happy, prosperous life.

11. A very sudden journey, with a pleasant fellow-traveler, and the result of the journey will be generally beneficial to your family.

12. You may regain that which you have lost with great perseverance and trouble,

13. You will soon receive news of the death of a relative for whom you have no very great respect, but who has included you in their will.

14. By venturing carefully, you will gain doubly, though you will suffer great hardship.

15. Your life will be filled with difficulties before you are comfortably settled.

16. Take care that you do not rush headlong into a new romance. If you do, family and friends may find fault with your new love. A careful examination of your heart is due at this point in your life.

17. Success in all ventures, whether they be about love, money or your career.

18. Let the chooser of this number persevere; for your schemes are good, and will succeed.

19. If you are not married, your potential mate is close at hand. If you are married, a child will be coming soon.

20. Your lover may not be the wittiest person around, but they are completely devoted to you.

21. Your marriage will be successful, and you will be very happy.

22. A drunken partner, bad success in trade, but the party will never be very poor, though always unhappy.

23. Do not neglect your lover; let your conduct command respect.

24. You have many friends, and will probably have a large and successful family.

25. Your travels will be prosperous, if you are prudent.

26. You have many enemies who will endeavor to make you unhappy.

27. The luck that is ordained for you, will be coveted by others.

28. Be very prudent in your conduct, as this number is very precarious and much depends upon yourself; it is generally good.

29. Beware, or you will be deceived by the person you are paying your attentions to.

30. You love one who is affectionate and true, and deserves respect.

31. You tend to be too cautious. Think carefully before you automatically refuse offers.

32. You will have bad luck for a short time, but be careful and your situation will very soon alter.

33. A fortune will be yours, but have patience and try not to be over anxious.

34. Alter you intentions or you will be sorry when it is too late.

35. You will have a rich, but jealous partner, and will live very uncomfortably.

36. You will have a sober, steady, and affectionate partner.

37. A very good fortune, sudden prosperity, and a large family.

38. The persons who choose this unlucky number, must carefully examine their life and actions, or justice will overtake them.

39. Remain among your, friends, then you will escape misfortune.

40. You will have an affectionate partner, but no family; and a large fortune.

41. If you have a fortune, be charitable; if but little, be frugal.

42. You will have a quarrel with your lover because of jealousy.

43. You must bear your losses with fortitude.

44. You will get a handsome, young, and wealthy partner.

45. When your conduct changes, your fortune will mend by marrying a rich partner.

46. You have taken up with the wrong crowd of friends. This will eventually cause you disgrace and unhappiness.

47. A large family of healthy children, give them learning, and they will honor their father and mother.

48. You will be very unfortunate at first, but persevere, and your schemes will be successful.

49. You have a number of secret enemies, who will try to do you an injury; be on your guard and you will prosper.

50. Your happiness will consist in doing good; later in life, you will look back fondly to these happy memories.

51. You will die alone and unloved. You have been selfish and missed out on a chance to find your true love.

52. Your lover will soon travel and will be very successful.

53. You will marry a person with whom you will have but little comfort.

54. This is a very lucky number; whatever you do, you will always prove successful.

55. After much misfortune, you will be pretty comfortable and happy.

56. Good conduct will produce much luck and happiness.

57. Your romance is not very happy. But, it could be if the two of you stopped thinking of only yourselves and work to make the other happy.

58. You have many lovers, but mind how you choose, or else you will suffer for it.

59. Your lover is on his way home, but he has met with severe losses.

60. You will receive a message announcing the loss of money.

61. You have a secret enemy, mind or he will do you harm.

62. Warns you against the evil consequences of idleness, either in yourself or partner.

63. Your partner will be very rich, but very neglectful.

64. Unless you work on your attitude, you will be very poor and miserable.

65. Sincere love from an upright heart will be rewarded.

68. You will marry someone whom you will be very unhappy.

67. Plenty of offers will happen before one is worthy of acceptance, be cautious how you make your choice.

68. You will play with the mouse until you lose it.

69. Take heed, you are being deceived by your lover.

70. You will meet with great trouble, you should have consulted your friends.

71. Beware, the person you love, does not love you.

72. If you marry in haste, you will be deceived, wait patiently, and you will be happy.

73. Hard work, hard fare, little joy, and much care.

74. You will be financially successful, but your marriage will not be so good.

75. Your partner will be very rich, but you will have no children.

76. You have a rival, be not deceived by false platitudes. Carefully look at your acquaintances and see who is jealous of you.

77. You will have many children, but you will be very poor.

78. It is time to stop fooling around and settle down with someone who really loves and cares about you.

79. Your spouse will be addicted to drinking and drugs.

80. Be honest and fair. You will triumph over your enemies.

81. You will have children, who, if you give them a good education, will make you happy.

82. You will fall into great difficulties, and if not careful, you will lose your partner and end up with alone and unhappy.

83. Stop worrying; the person you love is faithful, and you will be happy.

84. You must break off the connection you have formed, or you will be left unhappy.

85. Your lover is jealous, and will break up with you. But this is not necessarily a bad thing.

86. You will travel the world and see many strange and fascinating things. You may even find your life-partner on one of these trips.

87. You will get married, but it is still a few years away. So don't worry and enjoy your life.

88. Beware, you have a secret enemy who will try and do you harm.

89. If you are not careful, you will spend your life alone and unhappy.

90. Be very careful when choosing a possible romantic partner. You may not be making the best decisions when it comes to love.

91. The person you are paying your attentions to, is deceitful.

92. If you don't want to get married, then don't. You might be more happy being single.

93. You will live to a great age and be happy.

94. There is someone who is very much in love with you.

95. If you pay attention to the details, you may make a lot of money soon.

96. You are too deceitful to ever to be happy. Is this really how you want to spend your life?

97. A new romance is quickly winging its way to you. But be careful that you don't miss it as it comes by.

98. A shocking accident will happen to you, or to your children, which will cause great trouble.

99. Is your romantic partner being honest with you? Maybe not!

100. Your wishes will come true. Just make sure that your wishes will truly make you happy.

CHARMS AND MAGIC PROGNOSTICATIONS

Herewith I give a few mysterious magic formulas and prognostications, for the most part hitherto known only to wise old men and women, some of which I have had confided to me by learned astrologers, and a few were revealed to me by Madame Le Normand, a celebrated fortune-teller, **in whose predictions the Emperor Napoleon gave great confidence.**

TO PREPARE A LOVE POTION

The following substances must be gathered in silence when the full moon is in the heavens: *Three white rose leaves, three red rose leaves, three forget-me-nots, and five blossoms of Veronica.*

All these things you must place in a vessel, then pour upon them five hundred and ninety-five drops of clear Easter water, and place the vessel over the fire, or what is better still, over a spirit-lamp. This mixture must be allowed to boil for exactly the sixteenth part of an hour.

When it has boiled for the requisite length of time, remove it from the fire, and pour it into a flask. Cork it tightly, and seal it, and it will keep for years without losing its virtue.

That this potion is certain in its effect I myself will guarantee for I have gained more than thirty hearts by its help. Three drops swallowed by the person whose love you desire, will suffice.

FOR A GIRL TO ASCERTAIN IF SHE WILL EVER MARRY

Borrow a wedding-ring from a young married woman—the more recently she has been married the better—and do not tell her, or let her suspect your purpose; wear this ring on the third finger of your left hand at least three hours after sunset before you retire to rest.

When you are ready to go to bed, take half a sheet of pure white paper, with no rule marks or anything upon it, lay down the ring on the paper, and mark round it so as to make a circle exactly its size: you then write within the circle, "With this ring I hope to wed."

Write your name over the top, and your age underneath; fold the paper with a three-cornered love-letter fold, and put it under your pillow.

Before getting into bed, suspend the ring by a hair of your head over the pillow so that it will hang about six inches above your face. You will then dream of your future husband if you are ever to marry. If you dream of several men, the one whose appearance pleases you best will be the man. If you dream of women or girls exclusively, you will never marry. Sometimes it may happen that your dream is confused, and you have no clear recollection of it, or perhaps you may not dream at all, in which case you must continue this charm, by keeping the paper under your pillow for three nights: but the ring is not necessary after the first night.

THE STRAW SIGN

If you find a blade of straw lying in your chamber, you may expect a visitor that same day. If there is one grain upon the straw, the visitor will be a gentleman, if not, a lady.

THE SCISSOR OR KNIFE PROGNOSTIC

If a pair of scissors, a knife, or any other pointed instrument falls accidentally from your hand, and sticks in the floor, so that it remains upright, you may make every preparation for company, for be assured they will not fail to come.

THE CAT PORTENT

When the cat licks and trims herself, it is a sign of visitors, but this is probably known to most of my readers already,

SIGN OF VISITORS

Finally, a fourth sign of approaching visitors is the crying of the magpie. Magpies, as is well known, are the most inquisitive creatures upon the face of the earth. They fly from place to place, and hasten to everything. When they find out that any persons have concluded to pay you a visit, 'they fly to you at full speed, and bring you the news, for they are as chattering as they are inquisitive. They perch themselves upon your house, or upon a tree which may stand near it, or on the grass, and there sit and chatter until they think you must have understood them. Therefore, always give heed to these wise birds, for it is well to know when you are to expect visitors.

THE NEW MOON

On first seeing the new moon, if you happen to look at it over your right shoulder, you may make a silent wish, and you will realize it. If a girl thus observes the new moon, and desires to see her future husband, she must repeat to herself (so as not to be heard by any one) the following words:

New moon, new—pray let me see

Who my husband is to be:

The color of his hair,

The clothes he is to wear,

And the happy day that he'll wed me!

If she is to be married that year, she will positively see the man she is meant to be with before the wane of the full moon.

CARD CHARM

Draw all the face cards from the pack and put them into your stocking on a Friday night, placing the stocking under your pillow. You must find out the precise time the sun rises on Saturday morning, and at that moment draw a card. A king denotes a speedy marriage; a queen means delay or celibacy; a Jack is a seducer who will give you trouble. Diamonds are riches, hearts true love, spades thrift, and clubs poverty.

PSALM SPELL TO FIND HUSBAND OR WIFE

Psalm 111 is a favorite, as a person may acquire many friends by reciting it. Psalm 111:4 in particular is traditionally used in love spells. In order to find your true love, say out loud Psalm 111:4 once every Friday morning when you first arise in the morning. Repeat for the duration of the month.

Wait for one month, and then repeat. You should know your true love by the end of the second month.

He hath made his wonderful works to be remembered: the LORD is gracious and full of compassion. (Psalm 111:4)

MORE PSALM PRAYERS AND SPELLS

Healing Severe Headache or Backache

Psalm 3 was recited to treat a severe headache or a backache. It should be recited over rubbing oil, and then massaged into the head and/or back while praying. This Psalm was traditionally used in banishing troublesome and oppressive spirits who might be responsible for the physical discomfort.

Lord, how are they increased that trouble me! many are they that rise up against me. Many there be which say of my soul, There is no help for him in God. Selah. But thou, O LORD, art a shield for me; my glory, and the lifter up of mine head. I cried unto the LORD with my voice, and he heard me out of his holy hill. Selah. I laid me down and slept; I awaked; for the LORD sustained me. I will not be afraid of ten thousands of people, that have set themselves against me round about. Arise, O LORD; save me, O my God: for thou hast smitten all mine enemies upon the cheek bone; thou hast broken the teeth of the ungodly. Salvation belongeth unto the LORD: thy blessing is upon thy people. Selah. (Psalm 3)

A prayer such as the following may be added:

Lord of the world, may it please thee to be my physician and helper. Heal me and relieve me from my severe headache and backache, because I can find help only with thee and only with thee is counsel and action to be found. Amen. Selah.

Bringing Good Luck

Psalm 4 should be recited by someone who had been unlucky in spite of her/his good efforts. It ought to be recited three times just before sunrise.

Hear me when I call, O God of my righteousness: thou hast enlarged me when I was in distress; have mercy upon me, and hear my prayer. O ye sons of men, how long will ye turn my glory into shame? how long will ye love vanity, and seek after leasing? Selah. But know that the LORD hath set apart him that is godly for himself: the LORD will hear when I call unto him. Stand in awe, and sin not: commune with your own heart upon your bed, and be still. Selah. Offer the sacrifices of righteousness, and put your trust in the LORD. There be many that say, Who will shew us any good? LORD, lift thou up the light of thy countenance upon us. Thou hast put gladness in my heart, more than in the time that their corn and their wine increased. I will both lay me down in peace, and sleep: for thou, LORD, only makest me dwell in safety. (Psalm 4)

Adding this prayer:

May it please thee, oh Jehovah-jireh, to prosper my ways, steps, and doings. Grant that my desire be amply filled, and let my wishes be satisfied even this day for the sake of thy great and praise worthy name. Amen. Selah.

Get a Wish

If a person has a sincere wish, they should write that wish in large print on a small square of brown paper. This paper should be folded and burned in a fireproof bowl with sand. In the evening, Psalm 4 should be recited while the sand and ashes are scattered outside. The wind will carry the wish. The prayer above used in Bringing Good Luck can also be added by some.

Needing Financial Capital for One's Business

Psalm 4 should be recited by someone who needs investors and financial capital or economic capital in order to achieve his next goal in operating a business. It needs to be recited seven times before sunrise.

Adding this prayer, or similar prayer well suited:

May it please thee, oh Jehovah-jireh, to prosper my ways, steps, and doings. Let me find favor in the eyes of those investors who will grant my business proposal or petition even this day for the sake of thy great and praise worthy name. Amen. Selah.

Favorable Outcome When Dealing With Authorities

If a business does not prosper, particularly if the owner must deal with new government regulations, forms, etc, Psalm 5 should be recited daily at sunrise and at sunset until circumstances become more favorable.

Give ear to my words, O LORD, consider my meditation. Hearken unto the voice of my cry, my King, and my God: for unto thee will I pray. My voice shalt thou hear in the morning, O LORD; in the morning will I direct my prayer unto thee, and will look up. For thou art not a God that hath pleasure in wickedness: neither shall evil dwell with thee. The foolish shall not stand in thy sight: thou hatest all workers of iniquity. Thou shalt destroy them that speak leasing: the LORD will abhor the bloody and deceitful man. But as for me, I will come into thy house in the multitude of thy mercy: and in thy fear will I worship toward thy holy temple. Lead me, O LORD, in thy righteousness because of mine enemies; make thy way straight before my face. For there is no faithfulness in their mouth; their inward part is very wickedness; their throat is an open sepulchre; they flatter with their tongue. Destroy thou them, O God; let them fall by their own counsels; cast them out in the multitude of their transgressions; for they have rebelled against thee. But let all those that put their trust in thee rejoice: let them ever shout for joy, because thou defendest them: let them also that love thy name be joyful in thee. For thou, LORD, wilt bless the righteous; with favour wilt thou compass him as with a shield. (Psalm 5)

Successful Court Case Outcome

Psalm 5 can be recited by candlelight or lamplight just before sunrise and just after sunset for three days prior to the court case along with devoted prayers for favor from the judge.

The following prayer may also be recited with the holy name of Chanan-jah, meaning "Jah has favored."

Be merciful to me for the sake of thy great, adorable, and holy name. Chanan-jah, turn the favor of the judge to me, and grant that the judge may regard me with grace. Amen! Selah!

Healing Damaged Bones

The verse Psalm 6:2 should be recited for healing in particular bruises and aching bones. Recite the verse daily over an injured or broken bone as it heals.

Have mercy upon me, O Lord, for I am weak: O Lord, heal me, for my bones are vexed. (Psalm 6:2)

Breaking a Hex

To break a hex, frequently Psalm 7:1-10 is to be recited over a pot of well water, and poured out in the direction of wherever the hex supposedly originated.

O LORD my God, in thee do I put my trust: save me from all them that persecute me, and deliver me: Lest he tear my soul like a lion, rending it in pieces, while there is none to deliver. O LORD my God, If I have done this; if there be iniquity in my hands; If I have rewarded evil unto him that was at peace with me; (yea, I have delivered him that without cause is mine enemy:) Let the enemy persecute my soul, and take it; yea, let him tread down my life upon the earth, and lay mine honour in the dust. Selah. Arise, O LORD, in thine anger, lift up thyself because of the rage of mine enemies: and awake for me to the judgment that thou hast commanded. So shall the congregation of the people compass thee about: for their sakes therefore return thou on high. The LORD shall judge the people: judge me, O LORD, according to my righteousness, and according to mine integrity that is in me. Oh let the wickedness of the wicked come to an end; but establish the just: for the righteous God trieth the hearts and reins. My defence is of God, which saveth the upright in heart. (Psalm 7:1-10)

Repelling Terrestrial Dangers

Psalm 22:16-17 may be used to repel bad luck and dangers from water, wind, earth, or fire. The names of the four angels, "Tharsis," "Cherub," "Ariel," and "Seruph," should be written on the four arms of a cross drawn on paper. These are all angelic princes; they have great power in governing the elements of the earth. The verses of Psalm 22:16-17 must be written around the cross in a circle. Recite Psalm 22:16-17 each day devoutly to repel terrestrial dangers.

Whoever bears these words on paper, the Lord of the Earth, Jehovah-Adon Kal Ha'arets, will give the angels of the elements charge over that person to keep him or her safe in all his or her ways.

For dogs have compassed me: the assembly of the wicked have inclosed me: they pierced my hands and my feet. I may tell all my bones: they look and stare upon me. (Psalm 22:16-17)

Drawing Prosperity and Money

If you are wishing to draw prosperity and money, you should anoint yourself with an oil, such as olive oil mixed with bayberry oil, and recite Psalm 23 for seven mornings in a row upon arising from sleep. This Psalm is also good for success in gambling and winning the lottery.

The LORD is my shepherd; I shall not want. He maketh me to lie down in green pastures: he leadeth me beside the still waters. He restoreth my soul: he leadeth me in the paths of righteousness for his name's sake. Yea, though I walk through the valley of the shadow of death, I will fear no evil: for thou art with me; thy rod and thy staff they comfort me. Thou preparest a table before me in the presence of mine enemies: thou anointest my head with oil; my cup runneth over. Surely goodness and mercy shall follow me all the days of my life: and I will dwell in the house of the LORD for ever. (Psalm 23)

Divination and Dreams

Psalm 23 can also be recited when requesting an answer to a question in a dream. The dreamer will pray that the will of God be received in a dream, after reciting the Psalm just before the dreamer goes to sleep.

Honest Employment

If the whole Psalm 26 is pronounced over a small bottle of olive oil, the jar can be labeled "Honest Employment" and set aside. Next, anoint yourself lightly with this oil when seeking employment or looking for a job. *Judge me, O LORD; for I have walked in mine integrity: I have trusted also in the LORD; therefore I shall not slide. Examine me, O LORD, and prove me; try my reins and my heart. For thy lovingkindness is before mine eyes: and I have walked in thy truth. I have not sat with vain persons, neither will I go in with dissemblers. I have hated the congregation of evil doers; and will not sit with the wicked. I will wash mine hands in innocency: so will I compass thine altar, O LORD: That I may publish with the voice of thanksgiving, and tell of all thy wondrous works. LORD, I have loved the habitation of thy house, and the place where thine honour dwelleth.* (Psalm 26)

Overcoming Troublesome Spirits

Psalm 29 is to be recited ten times over water and seven palm leaves. The water is then poured out at the door of a house to cause a spirit to depart.

Give unto the LORD, O ye mighty, give unto the LORD glory and strength. Give unto the LORD the glory due unto his name; worship the LORD in the beauty of holiness. The voice of the LORD is upon the waters: the God of glory thundereth: the LORD is upon many waters. The voice of the LORD is powerful; the voice of the LORD is full of majesty. The voice of the LORD breaketh the cedars; yea, the LORD breaketh the cedars of Lebanon. He maketh them also to skip like a calf; Lebanon and Sirion like a young unicorn. The voice of the LORD divideth the flames of fire. The voice of the LORD shaketh the wilderness; the LORD shaketh the wilderness of Kadesh. The voice of the LORD maketh the hinds to calve, and discovereth the forests: and in his temple doth every one speak of his glory. The LORD sitteth upon the flood; yea, the LORD sitteth King for ever. The LORD will give strength unto his people; the LORD will bless his people with peace. (Psalm 29)

Recovering from Severe Illness

To speed a slow a recovery from a particularly nasty sickness, recite Psalm 30:11-12. In fact, all of Psalm 30 can be read to keep one safe from evil occurrences.

Hear, O LORD, and have mercy upon me: LORD, be thou my helper. Thou hast turned for me my mourning into dancing: thou hast put off my sackcloth, and girded me with gladness; To the end that my glory may sing praise to thee, and not be silent. O LORD my God, I will give thanks unto thee for ever. (Psalm 30:11-12)

Receiving Instruction in Dreams

Before a person goes to bed, they should recite Psalm 42:1-8 seven times in order to receive guidance, understanding, or information through a dream.

As the hart panteth after the water brooks, so panteth my soul after thee, O God. My soul thirsteth for God, for the living God: when shall I come and appear before God? My tears have been my meat day and night, while they continually say unto me, Where is thy God? When I remember these things, I pour out my soul in me: for I had gone with the multitude, I went with them to the house of God, with the voice of joy and praise, with a multitude that kept holyday. Why art thou cast down, O my soul? and why art thou disquieted in me? hope thou in God: for I shall yet praise him for the help of his countenance. O my God, my soul is cast down within me: therefore will I remember thee from the land of Jordan, and of the Hermonites, from the hill Mizar. Deep calleth unto deep at the noise of thy waterspouts: all thy waves and thy billows are gone over me. Yet the LORD will command his lovingkindness in the day time, and in the night his song shall be with me, and my prayer unto the God of my life. (Psalm 42:1-8)

Make Good Wishes Come True

In the evening, Psalm 40:5 should be recited by candlelight or lamplight along with someone's good wishes.

Many, O LORD my God, are thy wonderful works which thou hast done, and thy thoughts which are to us-ward: they cannot be reckoned up in order unto thee: if I would declare and speak of them, they are more than can be numbered. (Psalm 40:5)

Blessing When Moving to a New Home

To bring protection, good fortune, and blessing to the whole household just prior to moving into a new dwelling, Psalm 61 was recited.

Hear my cry, O God; attend unto my prayer. From the end of the earth will I cry unto thee, when my heart is overwhelmed: lead me to the rock that is higher than I. For thou hast been a shelter for me, and a strong tower from the enemy. I will abide in thy tabernacle for ever: I will trust in the covert of thy wings. Selah. For thou, O God, hast heard my vows: thou hast given me the heritage of those that fear thy name. Thou wilt prolong the king's life: and his years as many generations. He shall abide before God for ever: O prepare mercy and truth, which may preserve him. So will I sing praise unto thy name for ever, that I may daily perform my vows. (Psalm 61)

Protection from Attack

To avoid attack from unknown enemies (including magical attack) and accidents, one should recite Psalm 64.

Hear my voice, O God, in my prayer: preserve my life from fear of the enemy. Hide me from the secret counsel of the wicked; from the insurrection of the workers of iniquity: Who whet their tongue like a sword, and bend their bows to shoot their arrows, even bitter words: That they may shoot in secret at the perfect: suddenly do they shoot at him, and fear not. They encourage themselves in an evil matter: they commune of laying snares privily; they say, Who shall see them? They search out iniquities; they accomplish a diligent search: both the inward thought of every one of them, and the heart, is deep. But God shall shoot at them with an arrow; suddenly shall they be wounded. So they shall make their own tongue to fall upon themselves: all that see them shall flee away. And all men shall fear, and shall declare the work of God; for they shall wisely consider of his doing. The righteous shall be glad in the LORD, and shall trust in him; and all the upright in heart shall glory. (Psalm 64)

Blessings and Luck in New Endeavors

Psalm 65 should be recited for God's rich blessings and good luck in all of one's affairs. It could be recited while planting one's own vegetable garden or metaphorically planting the seed for any undertaking, as in starting at a new place of employment.

Praise waiteth for thee, O God, in Sion: and unto thee shall the vow be performed. O thou that hearest prayer, unto thee shall all flesh come. Iniquities prevail against me: as for our transgressions, thou shalt purge them away. Blessed is the man whom thou choosest, and causest to approach unto thee, that he may dwell in thy courts: we shall be satisfied with the goodness of thy house, even of thy holy temple. By terrible things in righteousness wilt thou answer us, O God of our salvation; who art the confidence of all the ends of the earth, and of them that are afar off upon the sea: Which by his strength setteth fast the mountains; being girded with power: Which stilleth the noise of the seas, the noise of their waves, and the tumult of the people. They also that dwell in the uttermost parts are afraid at thy tokens: thou makest the outgoings of the morning and evening to rejoice. Thou visitest the earth, and waterest it: thou greatly enrichest it with the river of God, which is full of water: thou preparest them corn, when thou hast so provided for it. Thou waterest the ridges thereof abundantly: thou settlest the furrows thereof: thou makest it soft with showers: thou blessest the springing thereof. Thou crownest the year with thy goodness; and thy paths drop fatness. They drop upon the pastures of the wilderness: and the little hills rejoice on every side. The pastures are clothed with flocks; the valleys also are covered over with corn; they shout for joy, they also sing. (Psalm 65)

Power for Strength and Protection

The holy name of Psalm 91 is El-Shaddai, which means God Almighty. Psalm 91 is traditionally credited to Moses. Psalm 91 can be recited against someone being afflicted or distressed by pestilence, danger, or an enemy. It is a boundary of protection which can be set around the family. For example, a woman who is afflicted by a rival for the affections of her husband may also recite this Psalm, keeping in mind the name of the LORD.

He that dwelleth in the secret place of the most High shall abide under the shadow of the Almighty. I will say of the LORD, He is my refuge and my fortress: my God; in him will I trust. Surely he shall deliver thee from the snare of the fowler, and from the noisome pestilence. He shall cover thee with his feathers, and under his wings shalt thou trust: his truth shall be thy shield and buckler. Thou shalt not be afraid for the terror by night; nor for the arrow that flieth by day; Nor for the pestilence that walketh in darkness; nor for the destruction that wasteth at noonday. A thousand shall fall at thy side, and ten thousand at thy right hand; but it shall not come nigh thee. Only with thine eyes shalt thou behold and see the reward of the wicked. Because thou hast made the LORD, which is my refuge, even the most High, thy habitation; There shall no evil befall thee, neither shall any plague come nigh thy dwelling. For he shall give his angels charge over thee, to keep thee in all thy ways. They shall bear thee up in their hands, lest thou dash thy foot against a stone. Thou shalt tread upon the lion and adder: the young lion and the dragon shalt thou trample under feet. Because he hath set his love upon me, therefore will I deliver him: I will set him on high, because he hath known my name. He shall call upon me, and I will answer him: I will be with him in trouble; I will deliver him, and honour him. With long life will I satisfy him, and shew him my salvation. (Psalm 91)

Overcome All Enemies

Whoever prays Psalm 100 seven days successively, seven times each day, will over come all his enemies, by praise of that divine name of power, Jah.

Make a joyful noise unto the LORD, all ye lands. Serve the LORD with gladness: come before his presence with singing. Know ye that the LORD he is God: it is he that hath made us, and not we ourselves; we are his people, and the sheep of his pasture. Enter into his gates with thanksgiving, and into his courts with praise: be thankful unto him, and bless his name. For the LORD is good; his mercy is everlasting; and his truth endureth to all generations. (Psalm 100)

He may also add this prayer:

Mighty, all-merciful, and compassionate, God, may it be pleasing to thy will to defend me from all enemies, for thine is the kingdom and the power and the glory forevermore. I will sing unto thee, sing praises to thine name: Jah. Hear me for the sake of thy most holy name, Jah! Hallelu-jah! Hallelu-jah! Hallelu-jah! Praise ye the LORD!

Drawing Success in Business

Traditionally, Psalm 114 is written with the holy name, Adonai, (Lord) on a clean piece of paper by anyone desiring success in his or her trade or business. This Psalm is then carried on one's person in a mojo bag prepared especially for that purpose. The divine title, "the God of Jacob," indicates that the Lord chooses one and passes by another.

When Israel went out of Egypt, the house of Jacob from a people of strange language; Judah was his sanctuary, and Israel his dominion. The sea saw it, and fled: Jordan was driven back. The mountains skipped like rams, and the little hills like lambs. What ailed thee, O thou sea, that thou fleddest? thou Jordan, that thou wast driven back? Ye mountains, that ye skipped like rams; and ye little hills, like lambs? Tremble, thou earth, at the presence of the Lord, at the presence of the God of Jacob; Which turned the rock into a standing water, the flint into a fountain of waters. (Psalm 114)

Protection from Violent or Sudden Death

Whoever prays Psalm 116 daily with devotion, trusting fully in God, will be safe from the danger of violent death; neither will that person be overtaken by a sudden death.

I love the LORD, because he hath heard my voice and my supplications. Because he hath inclined his ear unto me, therefore will I call upon him as long as I live. The sorrows of death compassed me, and the pains of hell gat hold upon me: I found trouble and sorrow. Then called I upon the name of the LORD; O LORD, I beseech thee, deliver my soul. Gracious is the LORD, and righteous; yea, our God is merciful. The LORD preserveth the simple: I was brought low, and he helped me. Return unto thy rest, O my soul; for the LORD hath dealt bountifully with thee. For thou hast delivered my soul from death, mine eyes from tears, and my feet from falling. I will walk before the LORD in the land of the living. I believed, therefore have I spoken: I was greatly afflicted. I said in my haste, All men are liars. What shall I render unto the LORD for all his benefits toward me? I will take the cup of salvation, and call upon the name of the LORD. I will pay my vows unto the LORD now in the presence of all his people. Precious in the sight of the LORD is the death of his saints. O LORD, truly I am thy servant; I am thy servant, and the son of thine handmaid: thou hast loosed my bonds. I will offer to thee the sacrifice of thanksgiving, and will call upon the name of the LORD. I will pay my vows unto the LORD now in the presence of all his people. In the courts of the LORD's house, in the midst of thee, O Jerusalem. Praise ye the LORD. (Psalm 116)

Empowerment Against Oppression

Psalm 129 should be recited in the morning against oppression and to block unfair treatment.

Many a time have they afflicted me from my youth, may Israel now say: Many a time have they afflicted me from my youth: yet they have not prevailed against me. The plowers plowed upon my back: they made long their furrows. The LORD is righteous: he hath cut asunder the cords of the wicked. Let them all be confounded and turned back that hate Zion. Let them be as the grass upon the housetops, which withereth afore it groweth up: Wherewith the mower filleth not his hand; nor he that bindeth sheaves his bosom. Neither do they which go by say, The blessing of the LORD be upon you: we bless you in the name of the LORD. (Psalm 129)

Obtaining Worldly Goods

To acquire "worldly goods" the portion of Psalm 132:12-18 is recited.

If thy children will keep my covenant and my testimony that I shall teach them, their children shall also sit upon thy throne for evermore. For the LORD hath chosen Zion; he hath desired it for his habitation. This is my rest for ever: here will I dwell; for I have desired it. I will abundantly bless her provision: I will satisfy her poor with bread. I will also clothe her priests with salvation: and her saints shall shout aloud for joy. There will I make the horn of David to bud: I have ordained a lamp for mine anointed. His enemies will I clothe with shame: but upon himself shall his crown flourish. (Psalm 132:12-18)

Give Praise

Psalm 150 is to be uttered in praise of the LORD for having received a favor or grace in answer to a prayer or having escaped a danger.

Praise ye the LORD. Praise God in his sanctuary: praise him in the firmament of his power. Praise him for his mighty acts: praise him according to his excellent greatness. Praise him with the sound of the trumpet: praise him with the psaltery and harp. Praise him with the timbrel and dance: praise him with stringed instruments and organs. Praise him upon the loud cymbals: praise him upon the high sounding cymbals. Let every thing that hath breath praise the LORD. Praise ye the LORD. (Psalm 150)

The joyous praise of the LORD in Psalm 150 can also turn sadness into glee.

THE SPIDER OMEN

It is considered an ill omen when one sees a spider in the morning. The earlier in the morning, and the larger the spider, the greater the evil which threatens you. It is indoors, however, and often in your bedroom, that the spider has this signification—out of doors, they forebode no harm.

The wood spider especially, is not much to be dreaded; what I have said above refers particularly to the house spider. Never, on any account, kill a wood spider. By such an act you would only draw upon yourself the hatred of the whole race of nature spirits, and sooner or later you will suffer from it.

When found in the evening, a spider signifies good luck. The smaller the spider, the greater the good fortune. I will here teach you the following rhyme:

"Araignée du matin, chagrin, araignée du soir, espoir."

(Seeing a spider in the morning brings bad luck, seeing a spider in the evening brings good luck.)

Little spiders have much less evil in them than the others, and those called daddy-long-legs are always messengers of good luck.

THE STRING TOKEN

If your shoe-tie or apron string breaks, your sweetheart is thinking of you.

SIGN WHEN YOUR RIGHT EAR TINGLES

If your right ear tingles, some one is speaking well of you. If the left ear tingles, some one is speaking ill of you. To find out who this some one is, you must call out aloud the names of your acquaintance, one after another. The name at which the tingling ceases is the name of the person. By that token, itches on different parts of your body can mean different things. For example, if your nose itches early in the morning, on that very day, you will hear some interesting news. Here is a very useful list of the divinatory meaning of itches.

Head - An advance in position and general good luck.

Right Ear - Someone is speaking well of you.

Left Ear - Someone is speaking ill of you.

Right Cheek - Someone is speaking well of you.

Left Cheek - Someone is speaking ill of you.

Right Eye or Eyebrow - Meeting or hearing from an old friend.

Left Eye or Eyebrow - A big disappointment.

Nose (inside) - Troubles and sorrows.

Nose (outside) - You will be kissed, cursed, annoyed, or meet a fool within the hour.

Lips - Someone is speaking disrespectfully about you.

Back of the neck - Illness of a relative.

Right Shoulder - Legacy.

Left Shoulder - Sorrow.

Right Elbow - Pleasant and exciting news. Sleeping with someone new before long.

Left Elbow - Bad news or losses but still sleeping with someone new before long.

Right Palm - Much money - scratch to your hearts content!

Left Palm - You will have to pay a debt - don't scratch it!

Spine - Disappointments.

Loins - Reconciliation after a quarrel or estrangement.

Stomach - A dinner invitation.

Thighs - A change of residence.

Right Knee - A happy journey. Kneeling in a strange place.

Left Knee - A trip beset with misfortune. Jealous of someone.

Shins - An unpleasant surprise.

Left Ankle - A marriage or paying out money.

Right Ankle - Receiving money - scratch away!

Feet - A difficult journey.

THE SIGNS OF A SNEEZE

If anyone tells you anything, and you are shortly after obliged to sneeze, you may be sure that what was told you is true. Another related to sneezes signifies the meaning of sneezes on any day of the week.

Sneeze on Monday, sneeze for fun,
Sneeze on Tuesday, meet someone
Sneeze on Wednesday, get a letter
Sneeze on Thursday, get something better
Sneeze on Friday, sneeze in sorrow
Sneeze on Saturday, see friends tomorrow
Sneeze on Sunday, bad luck for a week

It is interesting that in the way of Augury, sneezing should be held to such high regard. The ancient Egyptians regarded the head as a citadel or fortress in which the reasoning faculty abode. Hence they especially revered any function seemingly appertaining to so noble a portion of the body, and dignified even the insignificant act of sneezing by attributing to it auguries for good or evil, according to the position of the moon with reference to the signs of the zodiac. The Greeks and Romans also, by whom the most trivial occurrences of every-day life were thought to be omens of good fortune or the reverse, considered the phenomena of sneezing as not the least important in this regard. Homer tells us in the Odyssey that the Princess Penelope, troubled by the importunities of her suitors, prayed to the gods for the speedy return of her husband Ulysses. Scarcely was her prayer ended when her son Telemachus sneezed, and this event was regarded by Penelope as an intimation that her petition would be granted.

Aristotle said that there was a god of sneezing, and that when in Greece any business enterprise was to be undertaken, two or four sneezes were thought to be favorable. If more than four, the auspices were indifferent, while one or three rendered it hazardous to proceed. About this, however, there appears to have been no unvarying rule. Sneezing at a banquet was considered by the Romans to be especially ominous; and when it unfortunately occurred, some of the viands were brought back to the table and again tasted, as this was thought to counteract any evil effects. The Greeks considered that the brain controlled the function of sneezing. They were therefore as careful to avoid eating this portion of any animal as the Pythagoreans were to avoid beans as an article of diet.

It is related that just before the battle of Salamis, B.C. 480, and while Themistocles, the Athenian commander, was offering a sacrifice to the gods on the deck of his galley, a sneeze was heard on the right hand, which was hailed as a fortunate omen by Euphrantides the Soothsayer. Again, it happened once that while Xenophon was addressing his soldiers, referring to the righteousness of their cause and the consequent divine favor which might be expected, some one chanced to sneeze. Pausing in his address, the great general remarked that Jupiter had been pleased to send them a happy omen, and it seemed therefore but right to make an offering to the gods. Then, after all the company had joined in a hymn of thanksgiving, the sacrifice was made, and Xenophon continued with his exhortation.

Among the ancients sneezing to the right was considered fortunate and to the left unlucky. In some erotic verses with the title "Acme and Septimius," by the Roman poet, Catullus (B.C. 87-47), are these lines, twice repeated:

> *Love stood listening with delight,*
> *And sneezed his auspice on the right.*

The omens of sneezing were thought to be of especial significance in lovers' affairs, and indeed the classic poets were wont to say of beautiful women that Love had sneezed at their birth. The Italian poet, Propertius, while asserting his enduring affection for Cynthia, the daughter of the poet Hostius, thus apostrophizes the chief theme of his eulogies: "In thy new-born days, my life, did golden Love sneeze loud and clear a favoring omen."

The Egyptians, Greeks, and Romans regarded the act of sneezing as a kind of divinity or oracle, which warned them on various occasions as to the course they should pursue, and also foretold future good or evil.

Plutarch said that the familiar spirit or demon of Socrates was simply the sneezing either of the philosopher himself or of those about him. If any person in his company sneezed on his right hand, Socrates felt encouraged to proceed with the project or enterprise which he may have had in mind. But if the sneeze were on his left hand, he abandoned the undertaking. If he himself sneezed when he was doubtful whether or not to do anything, he regarded it as evidence in the affirmative; but if he happened to sneeze after any work was already entered upon, he immediately desisted. The demon, we are told, always notified him by a slight sneeze whenever his wife Xantippe was about to have a scolding fit, so that he was thus enabled opportunely to absent himself. And in so doing Socrates appears to have given proof, were any needed, of his superior wisdom; for Xantippe had been known to upset the supper-table in her anger, and that, too, when a guest was present.

On a column in the garden of the House of the Faun, at Pompeii, there is a Latin inscription which may be freely translated as follows:

Victoria, good luck to thee and wherever thou wilt, sneeze pleasantly.

Clement of Alexandria, in a treatise on politeness, characterizes sneezing as effeminate and as a sign of intemperance. Probably the only Biblical reference to the subject of sneezing is in 2 Kings iv. 35, where the son of the Shunamite sneezed seven times and then revived at the prayer of Elisha.

Hor-Apollo, in his treatise on Egyptian hieroglyphics, says that the inhabitants of ancient Egypt believed that the capacity for sneezing was in inverse ratio to the size of the spleen; and they portrayed the dog as the personification of sneezing and smelling, because they believed that that animal had a very small spleen. On the other hand, they held that animals with large spleens were unable to sneeze, smell, or laugh, that is, to be open, blithe, or frank-hearted.

The function of the spleen in the animal economy is not fully understood to-day. If the above theory were correct, we should expect that the removal of a dog's spleen would incite excessive sternutation and render more acute the sense of smell, whereas the only marked result of the operation is a voracious appetite. The theory is certainly unique, as well as illogical and absurd.

St. Augustine wrote that, in his time, so prevalent was faith in the omens of sneezing that a man would return to bed if he happened to sneeze while putting on his shoes in the morning.

The learned English prelate, Alcuin (735-804), expressed the opinion that sneezings were devoid of value as auguries except to those who placed reliance in them. But he further remarked that "it was permitted to the evil spirit, for the deceiving of persons who observe these things, to cause that in some degree prognostics should often foretell the truth."

In an ancient Anolo-Saxon sermon a copy of which is in the library of Cambridge University, England, reference is made to certain superstitions existing among the Saxons before their conversion to Christianity. The writer says: "Every one who trusts in divinations, either by fowls or by sneezings, or by horses or dogs, he is no Christian, but a notorious apostate."

Sneezing at the commencement of an undertaking, whether it be an important enterprise or the most commonplace act, has usually been accounted unlucky. Thus, according to a modern Teutonic belief, if a man sneeze on getting up in the morning, he should lie down again for another three hours, else his wife will be his master for a week. So likewise the pious Hindu, who may perchance sneeze while beginning his morning ablutions in the river Ganges, immediately recommences his prayers and toilet; and among the Alfoorans or aborigines of the island of Celebes in the Indian archipelago, if one happens to sneeze when about leaving a gathering of friends, he at once resumes his seat for a while before making another start.

When a native of the Banks Islands, in Polynesia, sneezes, he imagines that some one is calling his name, either with good or evil intent, the motive being shown by the character of the sneeze. Thus a gentle sneeze implies kindly feeling on the part of the person speaking of him, while a violent paroxysm indicates a malediction.

In the latter case he resorts to a peculiar form of divination in order to ascertain who it is that curses him. This consists in raising the arms above the head and revolving the closed fists one around the other. The revolution of the fists is the question, "Is it such an one?" Then the arms are thrown out, and the answer, presumably affirmative, is given by the cracking of the elbow-joints.

In Scotland even educated people have been known to maintain that idiots are incapable of sneezing, and hence, if this be true, the inference is clear that the act of sternutation is prima facie evidence of the possession of a certain degree of intelligence.

British nurses used to think that infants were under a fairy spell until they sneezed. "God sain the bairn," exclaimed an old Scotch nurse when her little charge sneezed at length, "it's no a warlock."

The Irish people also entertain similar beliefs. Thus in Lady Wilde's "Ancient Cures, Charms, and Usages of Ireland" (p. 41) is to be found the following description of a magical ceremony for the cure of a fairy-stricken child. A good fire is made, wherein is thrown a quantity of certain herbs prescribed by the fairy women; and after a thick smoke has risen, the child is carried thrice around the fire while an incantation is repeated and holy water is sprinkled about liberally. Meantime all doors must be closed, lest some inquisitive fairy enter and spy upon the proceedings; and the magical rites must be continued until the child sneezes three times, for this looses the spell, and the little one is permanently redeemed from the power of witches.

Among other peoples, the sneeze of a young child has a certain mystic significance, and is intimately associated with its prospective welfare or ill-luck. When, therefore, a Maori infant sneezes, its mother immediately recites a long charm of words. If the sneeze occurs during a meal, it is thought to be prognostic of a visit, or of some interesting piece of news; whereas in Tonga it is deemed an evil token.

So, too, among the New Zealanders, if a child sneeze on the occasion of receiving its name, the officiating priest at once holds to its ear the wooden image of an idol and sings some mystic words.

In a note appended to his *"**Mountain Bard**,"* the Ettrick Shepherd says, regarding the superstitions of Selkirkshire: "When they sneeze in first stepping out of bed in the morning, they are thence certified that strangers will be there in the course of the day, in numbers corresponding to the times they sneeze."

It was a Flemish belief that a sneeze during a conversation proved that what one said was the truth, a doctrine which must have commended itself to snuff-takers.

In Shetlandic and Welsh folk-lore the sneeze of a cat indicates cold north winds in summer and snow in winter; and the Bohemians have an alleged infallible test for recognizing the Devil, for they believe that he must perforce sneeze violently at sight of a cross.

According to a Chinese superstition, a sneeze on New Year's Eve is ominous for the coming year; and, to offset this, the sneezer must visit three families of different surnames, and beg from each a small tortoise-shaped cake, which must be eaten before midnight.

In Turkistan, when a person to whom a remark is addressed sneezes, it is an asseveration that the opinion or statement is correct, just as if the person accosted were to exclaim, "That is true!" In the same country three sneezes are unlucky. When, also, any one hiccoughs, it is etiquette to say, "You stole something from me," and this phrase at such times is supposed to produce good luck.

The Japanese attach significance to the number of tunes a man sneezes. Thus, one sneeze indicates that some one is praising him, while two betoken censure or disparagement; a triple sneeze is commonplace, and means simply that a person has taken cold. In Mexico, also, it was formerly believed either that somebody was speaking evil of one who sneezed, or that he was being talked about by one or more persons.

Sussex people are prejudiced against cats which develop sneezing proclivities, for they believe that, when a pet feline sneezes thrice, it augurs ill for the health of the household, and is premonitory of influenza and bronchial affections.

In an interesting article in *Macmillan's Magazine*, entitled "From the Note-book of a Country Doctor," a physician practicing in a remote part of

Cornwall tells of a peculiar cure for deafness which recently came to his notice.

One of his patients, an elderly woman whose name was Grace Rickard, complained that she could no longer hear the grunting of her pigs, a sound which, from childhood, had roused her from sleep in the early morning. The doctor was obliged to tell her that the difficulty was due to advancing years.

A short time after, on calling at her house, he found her sitting before the fire with a piece of board in her lap, and deeply absorbed in thought. Just as the door opened, she exclaimed: "Lord, deliver me from my sins," and this petition was followed by a peculiar noise which sounded like an abortive sneeze. "Don't be frited, zur," she said, "'tes aunly a sneeze." "It's the oddest sneeze I ever heard," said the doctor; "why can't you sneeze in the ordinary way?" "So I do, when I can," she explained; "but now 'tes got up to nine times running, and wherever to get nine sneezes from is moor'n I knaw."

It appeared that Grace was making trial of an infallible cure for deafness, the necessary apparatus for which consisted of a piece of board and some stout pins. One of the latter is stuck into the board every morning, the patient's forefingers being crossed over the pin, while the pious ejaculation above mentioned is repeated simultaneously with a vigorous sneeze. On the next morning two pins must be stuck in the board, the petition and sneeze being once repeated; on the following morning three pins, three prayers, and three sneezes, and so on up to nine times.

One sneeze, a wish
Two sneezes, a kiss
Three sneezes, a disappointment
Four sneezes, a letter

THE DEATH-TICK

If you hear a wood-tick or death-watch ticking anywhere in the house, you must try to get rid of it as soon as possible, or you will speedily hear of a death which will greatly afflict you.

THE CRICKET

If there is a cricket in the house, be careful on no account to disturb it. This is because a cricket in your house tells of money on its way or some other prosperity coming.

On the other hand, many American Indians believe that the cricket is a sign of bad luck. Seeing a cricket in ones house means that bad prayers or bad wishes are being made against you. As a result, the offending cricket needs to be caught, burned and prayed against.

THE CANDLE TOKEN

When a large red token forms in the flame of a candle-wick, it signifies that the one who first sees it will soon receive a message.

THE STAR AUGUR

When you are out of doors on a starlit evening, and shooting stars appear, turn your face upward to the stars, and utter in a whisper the wish nearest your heart. If a star shoots while you do this, you may be sure that the wish will be fulfilled.

THE CROW SIGN

If you wish to know how matters will go with you during the year, you must take good heed of the first crow that you see in the spring. If, when you first see it, it is flying, it signifies that you will take a journey that will be longer or shorter, according to the distance which the bird flies before it alights. It may also signify a complete change of abode, perhaps by a wedding. If you first see the bird sifting, you will remain at home; if upon one leg, fortune will not smile upon you. The number of crows you see is also significant for the upcoming year.

One Crow for sorrow,
Two Crows for mirth;
Three Crows for a wedding,
Four Crows for a birth;
Five Crows for silver,
Six Crows for gold;

Seven Crows for a secret, not to be told;
Eight Crows for heaven,
Nine Crows for hell;
And ten Crows for the devils own self.

A CHARM AGAINST NIGHTMARES

If you wish to be secure against the nightmare in your sleep, place your shoes side by side upon the floor, at the foot of the bed, so that the toes will point not toward the bed, but in the contrary direction, as if they were going from it.

WHAT A PRICK IN THE FINGER SIGNIFIES

If you are sewing upon a new dress, apron, etc. and you prick your finger with the needle so as to bring blood, it is a sign that when you first wear the garment you will receive many kisses. Each pricked finger has a meaning. The right hand means work, the left hand means - heart. Pricking your thumb means joy. Then it goes: boredom, love, a letter, a parting.

THE HAIR SPELL

If you wish any person to think of yon, pluck a hair from your head, and blow it out into the air toward that quarter of the heavens in which the person lives, while, at the same time, you call out the name of this person three times, at the top of your voice. During this you must be entirely alone, and must have thought intently upon the person for, at least, a quarter of an hour beforehand. At the same instant he will experience a strange unearthly shudder or thrill, and all thoughts will turn irresistibly toward you.

HOW TO DETERMINE THE LUCKY AND UNLUCKY DAYS OF ANY MONTH OF THE YEAR

Ascertain from the Almanac the day on which a full moon occurs, and count the number of days from that to the end of the month: you then multiply the number of days in the month by the number ascertained as above, and the total will give you the lucky days: if the total happens to be say 516, the lucky days of that month would be the 5th and 16th. Suppose that instead of 516, the total should be 399: as neither of these figures can be paired, the lucky days from that total are the 3rd and 6th, and the 6th would be considered doubly lucky.

The unlucky days are determined in precisely the same manner, by multiplying the number of days in the month by the number which had passed previous to a full moon. After working out your list of lucky days, in the manner above described, you must then test them, in order to be sure that there are no opposing influences. You can do this by calculating the unlucky days. Should you find that any day of the month which was designated as lucky came also m the list of unlucky days, the latter preponderates, and you must strike it from the lucky list.

This plan of demonstrating lucky and unlucky days is very ancient, and has been, tested to such an extent that it is considered accurate by most astrologers. In old times, before the mass of the people understood much about figures, the professional fortune-tellers demanded a large fee for casting the lucky days of any month, which they accomplished in the manner above described. Lucky marriage days for girls were cast in the same manner, except that the age of the girl was used as the multiplicator, or multiplier. Instead of the number of days in the month. The result was determined similarly, and also by a test of the unlucky days. Thus, if a girl is 18 years old, and thinks of marrying in October, she takes up an Almanac and ascertains the day of the full moon in that month.

It occurs on the 24th, and there are 31 days in the month: this leaves 7 for the multipher. She multiplies this by her age, 13, and the result is 106, which shows the lucky days in that month for her to marry are the 10th and 6th, unless they are destroyed by the test, which is determined as follows: There are 23 days before the 24th, and she must multiply 23 by 18, which gives 414, and shows that the 4th and 14th are the only unlucky days for her to marry; and as they do not conflict with the lucky days, the 6th and 10th may be considered as genuine lucky days for that month, reckoning the moon to have fulled on the 24th. In determining her age, she should reckon any period over half a year a full year.

THE MOON AND THE LUCK IT BRINGS

People of all ages have looked upon the moon as a provider of good and bad luck, and most of us have probably noticed that it has influenced our actions, at times. Here are some of the beliefs that are centuries old.

If you see a new moon over your right shoulder, it means that you will experience good luck all the month.

If you have money in your pocket and you meet the new moon face to face, turn the money over and you will not run short of money that month.

It is unlucky to see the new moon through glass. If you do, go out of doors, curtsey three times to the moon and turn some silver in your hand.

This will break the spell which will be cast over you if you do not do as directed. There is one little point, connected with this superstition, which has set us thinking. What of all those individuals who wear glasses? We do not know the answer.

There is a strongly prevalent idea that everything falling to the lot of man when the moon is waxing will increase or prosper; but things decrease and do not prosper when the moon is on the wane.

Irish colleens were wont to drop on their knees when they first caught sight of the new moon, and say, "Oh, moon, leave us as well as you have found us." And, long ago, Yorkshire maidens "did worship the new moon on their bent knees, kneeling upon the earth-cast stone."

If the full moon known as the Harvest Moon appears watery, it is an ill sign for the harvest. (The Harvest Moon is due about the middle of September.)

If the moon shows a silver shield, be not afraid to reap your field: but if she rises haloed round, soon we'll tread on deluged ground.

If the moon changes on a Sunday there will be a flood before the month is out.

A Saturday moon, if it comes once in seven years, comes too soon.
A fog and a small moon bring an easterly wind soon.
In the waning of the moon,
Cloudy morning: fair afternoon.
Pale moon doth rain; red moon doth blow,
White moon doth neither rain nor snow.
When the moon's halo is far, the storm is n'ar (near).

131

When the moon's halo is n'ar, the storm is far.
It has long been a custom for girls to go to the nearest stile, to turn their
back on the first new moon after Midsummer and to chant these verses:
All hail, new moon, all hail to thee.
I prithee, good moon, reveal to me,
This night, who shall my true love be.
Who he is and what he wears,
And what he does all months and years.

If she were to be married in the course of the next twelve months, the moon answered her questions during her sleep of the same evening.

In many parts of the country it is supposed that, on Christmas Eve, the moon will help maidens to find out when they are to be married. The plan is for a maiden to borrow a silk handkerchief from a male relation and to take it and a mirror to some sheet of water, while the night is dark. She must go quite alone; but the sheet of water may be an unromantic pail, full to the brim, stationed at the bottom of the garden. As soon as the moon shows itself, the maiden places the flimsy piece of silk in front of her eyes, and, by holding the mirror half towards the moon and half towards the water, it is possible for her to see more than a pair of reflections. The number of reflections are the months which will ensue before her wedding bells ring out.

We recently came across the following information in a document quite three hundred years old:

"The first, second and third days of the moon's age are lucky for buying and selling; the seventh, ninth and eleventh are lucky for engagements and marriage; the sixteenth and twenty-first are not lucky for anything."

The same document affirmed that:

"A baby born before the new moon is twenty-four hours old is sure to be lucky. Anything lost during the second twenty-four hours of the moon's age is sure to be found. All things begun on the fifth twenty-four hours will turn out successfully. A dream experienced on the eighth twenty -four hours must come true."

TELL YOUR FORTUNE WITH DICE AND DOMINOES

This is a certain and innocent way of finding out common occurrences about to take place. Take three dice, shake them well in the box with your left hand, and then cast them out on a board or table, on which you had previously drawn a circle with chalk, but never throw on Monday or Wednesday.

Three — a pleasing surprise.

Four — a disagreeable one.

Five — a stranger who will prove a friend.

Six — loss of property.

Seven — undeserved scandal.

Eight — merited reproach.

Nine — a wedding.

Ten — a christening, at which some important event will occur to you.

Eleven — a death that concerns you.

Twelve — a letter, speedily.

Thirteen — tears and sighs.

Fourteen— a new admirer.

Fifteen — beware that you are not drawn into some trouble or plot.

Sixteen — a pleasant journey.

Seventeen — you will either be on the water, or have dealing with those belonging to it, to your advantage.

Eighteen— *a great profit, rise in life, or some most desirable good will happen almost immediately; for the answers to the dice are always fulfilled within nine days.*

To show the same number twice at one trial, shows news from abroad, be the number what they may. If the dice rollover the circle, the number thrown goes for nothing, but the occurrence shows sharp words, and if they fall to the floor it is blows; in throwing out the dice, if one remains on the top of the other, it is a present, of which I would have the females take care.

DOMINOES

Lay them with their faces on the table, and shuffle them; then draw one, and see the number. Never play on a Friday.

Double-six — receiving a handsome sum of money.

Six-five — going to a public amusement.

Six-four — law-suits.

Six-three — ride in a coach.

Six-two — present of clothing.

Six-one — you will soon perform a friendly action.

Six-blank — guard against scandal, or you will suffer by your inattention.

Double-five — a new abode to your advantage.

Five-four — a fortunate speculation.

Five-three — a visit from a superior.

Five-two — a water-party.

Five-one — a love intrigue.

Five-blank — a funeral, but not of a relation.

Double-four — drinking liquor at a distance.

Four-three — a false alarm at your house.

Four-two — beware of thieves or swindlers. — Ladies, take notice of this; it means more than it says.

Four-one — trouble from creditors.

Four-blank — receive a message from an angry friend.

Double-three — sudden wedding, at which you will be vexed.

Three-two — buy no lottery tickets, not enter into any game of chance, or you will lose.

Three-one — a great discovery at hand.

Three-blank — an illegitimate child.

Double-two — you will be plagued by a jealous partner.

Two-one — you will mortgage or pledge some property very soon.

Double-one — you will soon find something to your advantage in the street or road.

Double-blank — the worst presage in all the set of dominoes; you will soon meet trouble from a quarter for which you are quite unprepared.

It is useless for any person to draw more than three dominoes at one time of trial, or in one and the same month, as they will only deceive themselves; shuffle the dominoes each time of choosing ; to draw the same domino twice makes the answer stronger.

THE ANISEED CHARM: OR, HOW TO SUCCEED IN ANY GREAT UNDERTAKING

If you are going on any great undertaking and wish to succeed in it, you should anoint your head and feet with aniseed, and cross your face and chest with red chalk; cut three locks of your hair from the back of your head, make a good fire with coke or coal, stand in front of the same, and commit the hair to the flames, repeating the following verse three times without once drawing breath:

O sweet aniseed do assist me,
To succeed in this, and I will bless thee,
For a great undertaking I want your aid.
Grant me the same, and my fortune is made.

Watch the fire till the last spark has expired, go to bed at midnight, rise at four, and well cleanse your skin from the anointment, go to bed again until five o'clock, then get up and commence operations, and you will be sure to succeed.

JUDGMENTS DRAWN FROM THE MOON'S AGE

1. A child born within twenty-one hours after the new moon will be fortunate and live to a good old age; whatever is dreamt on this day will be fortunate and pleasant to the dreamer; various undertakings will succeed on this day.

2. This is a very lucky day for discovering things lost or hidden; the child born on this day will thrive, but the dreams are not to be depended upon.

3. A child born on this day will be fortunate through persons in power, and all dreams will prove true.

4. This day is bad; persons failing on this day rarely recover; the dreams will have no effect.

5. This day is favorable to begin a good work, and the dreams will be tolerably successful; the child born on this day will be vain and deceitful.

6. The dreams of this day will not immediately come to pass; and the child born will not live long.

7. Do not tell your dreams on this day; if sickness befall you on this day you will soon recover; the child born will live long, but have many troubles.

8. Dreams of this day will come to pass; business begun on this day will prosper, and anything lost will be found.

9. This day differs little from the former, the child born on this day will acquire great riches and honor.

10. This day is likely to be fatal; those who fall sick will rarely recover; the child born on this day will fee devoted to religion, and of an engaging form and manner; if a female, she will possess an uncommon share of wisdom and learning; this day is good to begin a journey, to marry, or to engage in business.

11. Dreams on this day are fortunate; and the child born will live long, and be very sensible ; but a person who falls sick on this day rarely recovers.

12. Dreams on this day will quickly prove true.

13. If you ask a favor on this day, it will be granted.

14. The sickness that befalls a person on this day is likely to prove mortal; what was lost yesterday may be found today.

15. The child born on this day will be of ill manners and unfortunate; it is a good day for dealing in merchandise.

16. The child born on this day will be foolish; it is an unlucky day to marry, or to begin any kind of business on.

17. The child born on this day will be very valiant, but will suffer hardships; if a female, she will be chaste and industrious, and live respected to a great age.

18. This day is dangerous; the child born will be dishonest.

19. Dreams on this day will be vain and untrue; the child born will grow up healthy and strong, but be of a selfish and ungentle.

20. The child born will be fortunate, and of a cheerful countenance, religious, and much beloved; any kind of business begun on this day will be unfortunate.

21. The child born on this day will be of an ungovernable temper, forsake his friends, wander in a foreign land, and be unhappy through life; it is a happy day to marry on; and all business begun on this day will be successful.

22. The child born on this day will be wicked, meet with many dangers, and come to an untimely end; it is a very unfortunate day, and threatens everything with disappointment and crosses; whoever falls sick on this day seldom recovers.

23. Dreams on this day are certain; and the child born on this day will be rich and greatly esteemed.

24. This day is favorable for dreams; and the child born will be of a sweet and amiable disposition.

25. This day is bad for dreams, and those who fall sick on it, are in great danger; the child born on this day will be its parents' delight, but will not live to any great age.

26. This day is good for dreams, but children born on it will experience many hardships, though in the end, they may turn out happily.

27. This is a very unfortunate day to look for anything that is lost, but a child born on this day will make a great stir in the world, either as a statesman, soldier, physician, or clergyman.

28. A child born upon this day will live to be a rich and truly good man if born before noon, but if born after that hour, it is to be feared that he will be dissipated or worthless.

29. Dreams on this day are not worth a moment's attention, for rest assured they will never be fulfilled. Never buy a lottery ticket on this day.

OTHER MOON LORE

It is lucky to see the first sliver of a new Moon "clear of the brush," or unencumbered by foliage.

It is lucky to own a rabbit's foot, especially if the rabbit was killed in a cemetery by a cross-eyed person at the dark of the Moon.

It is lucky to hold a moonstone in your mouth at the full Moon; it will reveal the future.

It is lucky to have a full Moon on the "Moon day" (Monday).

It is lucky to expose your newborn to the waxing Moon. It will give the baby strength.

It is lucky to move into a new house during the new Moon; prosperity will increase as the Moon waxes.

It is unlucky to see the first sliver of a new Moon through a window; you'll break a dish.

It is unlucky to point at the new Moon or view any Moon over your shoulder.

It is unlucky to sleep in the moonlight, or worse, be born in the moonlight.

It is unlucky to see "the old Moon in the arms of the new" or the faint image of the full disk while the new crescent Moon is illuminated, especially if you're a sailor. Storms are predicted.

It is unlucky to have a full Moon on Sunday. (Some say Saturday.)

In some cultures it is believed if you make a wish on the new moon when it goes thru the phases and returns to the new moon your wish will come true.

The Egyptians believed that the moon was impregnated by the son and then she let herself scatter among the earth. They called the moon "mother of the world," or the mother of the human species.

It is commonly believed that one that sleeps with bright moonlight shining directly upon him will become mentally defective.

It was believed that the full moon caused the mentally afflicted to be more upset. In time the work Lunatic, from Luna meaning moon, and tic meaning struck, evolved from this belief.

When a person sees the new moon for the first time they are to bow to it three times or three times three in honor of the ancient Egyptian Trinity, Osiris, Isis, and Horus, (the father, mother, and son).

To see the thin crescent over ones left shoulder is lucky.

People believed the moon was made of silver, so to ask the moon for help for something they would jingle the change in their pockets as they gazed at its glory.

The new moon is a time for planting, courtship, the starting of new business ventures or trip, cutting the hair and fingernail to effect a better growth, and so on.

According to Rumanian myth, the Sun had an incestuous desire for his sister, Moon. To avoid meeting her brother, Moon went about only at night when she could not be seen. To discourage him, she also made ugly marks on her face.

Girls are warned not to stare at the moon or lay in the moonlight, or they will be impregnated by the moon and will give birth to a monster.

It is unlucky to view the first new moon thru glass or thru a tree, also unlucky to point at the moon. At first sight of the new moon one should turn a silver coin in his purse or pocket and make a wish.

It is said that if a young girl holds a silk hankie at the face of the full moon, desiring to know when she will be married, the number of moons appearing will indicate the number of years she shall wait.

Pigs killed when the moon is waxing will yield bacon richer and fatter.

An English tradition holds that a housewife seeing the new moon for the first time should run quickly to her bedroom and turn a bed.

To cure warts catch some moonbeams in a metal basin and wash your hands in them saying "I was my hands in thy dish O man in the moon, do grant my wish, And come and take this away"

A ring around the moon is an omen of rain or snow.

You will fail if you try to commit robbery on the third day of a full moon. Children born on the full moon will be strong,

New moon on a Saturday or Sunday is bad luck and is an omen of rain.

To find out about your romantic prospects, glance at the New moon over your right shoulder and say:

New moon, new moon, true and bright,

If I have a lover let me dream of him tonight.

If I am to marry far, let me hear a bird cry;

If I am to marry near, let me hear a cow low;

If I am to marry never, let me hear a hammer knock.

In astrology, it is the Moon's association with water that dominates its influence. According to Ptolemy: "The Moon has a higher degree of her power in moistening because of proximity to the earth (quite obviously) and the exhalation of moisture."

Time-honored folklore claims that the waxing and waning of the Moon reflects a monthly cycle of water content in the Earth and its produce, with the full Moon representing the time of greatest moisture.

In gardening lore, the first quarter of the waxing Moon is the ideal time to plant seeds, repot plants, sow lawns, etc., but if the weather is particularly dry the gardener is advised to plant his seeds at the full Moon, when conditions are likely to be more moist.

Full Moons are also favored for harvesting plants that need to be rich in moisture content, such as grapes, tomatoes, and strawberries, while plants that produce "below the ground," such as potatoes and carrots, are best planted during the "dark of the Moon." The waning Moon is the time for killing weeds, cutting back dead growth, harvesting root vegetables and drying herbs, flowers and fruit.

Many omens concerning a strange lunar appearance warn of excess of moisture through floods or stormy weather. A halo around the Moon, for instance, is an ancient sign of rain. The smaller the halo, the higher the likelihood of rain. If there are stars in the halo some omens say that it will rain for as many days as there are stars, others that the rain will come after so many days.

The Moon on its back (when its horns point upwards) is said to hold water and presages a dry spell. In a general sense, it is an unfortunate omen which is sometimes taken as an augury of death.

Another omen claims that if the first crescent of the new Moon appears with its lower horn obscured, stormy weather is indicated in the first phase of the Moon. If the obscuration is in the middle of the Moon, the storm will occur around the time of the new Moon. If the upper horn is affected, the storm will come during the wane of the Moon. If you are not sure how to recognize a waxing or waning Moon from its appearance, remember that the waxing Moon grows larger from right to left. It is called the "right-hand Moon" because the curve of the crescent corresponds to the curve between the right-hand index finger and the thumb. Similarly, a waning Moon diminishes from right to left and is known as a "left-hand Moon" because of its correspondence with the curve on the left hand.

Another lunar indication of floods is a "Blue Moon," the term used when two full Moons fall in the same calendar month. This occurs, on average, once every two and a half years.

New Moons can also indicate bad weather. Sometimes, when a new Moon occurs on a clear night, a faint, golden outline of the full Moon can be seen as a continuation of the bright crescent. Traditional folklore refers to this as the "Old Moon in the New Moon's arms," a phenomenon created by earthshine — the reflection of light from the Earth back onto the surface of the Moon. Old customs take this to be the sign of a storm or misfortune; as one old ballad goes:

> Late, Late yester' ev'n I saw the new Moon
> wi' the old Moon in her arm
> and I fear, I fear, my dear master
> that we shall come to harm.

Another omen claims that if the new Moon is high in Northern latitude, it brings cold or unpleasant weather, but if far south, it presages a period of fair weather.

Despite the apparent risk of rain, many ancient festivals were timed for the period of the full Moon, partly for esoteric purposes, because it represented the fruition of the month, but mainly for practical purposes, because it was of course the time of greatest nighttime illumination. For example, the Jewish Passover is celebrated at the full Moon, and the Christian Easter (which sets the dates of later festivals) occurs on the first Sunday following the first full Moon after the Sun's return to the vernal equinox – delayed until the Sunday, the day of the Sun, since Easter is intrinsically connected to the resurrection of the Sun as it regains its strength in spring.

The appearance of the full Moon at the time near the Sun's passage of the equinoxes can be particularly impressive, because of its size and golden illumination. The full Moon nearest to the September equinox is known as the 'Harvest Moon' because it appears large and bright in the early evening for several nights in a row, giving farmers valuable extra time to gather in their harvest.

Although many myths refer to the Moon as a feminine influence, some ancient civilizations considered the Moon a masculine deity, whose role was to structure society as a measurer and recorder of time.

Folklore also continues to speak of the "Man in the Moon," who is often described as carrying a bundle of twigs or a bucket and who is generally reported to be a thief or tramp, transported to the Moon in punishment for some criminal or immoral activity.

One common folklore claims he was a beggar, whose crime was to gather firewood on Sunday, and whose punishment therefore was to live a perpetual "Monday" on the Moon.

USING THE MOON TO PREDICT THE WEATHER

In the wane of the Moon, a cloudy morning bodes a fair afternoon.

If the crescent Moon holds its points upward, able to contain water, it predicts a dry spell.

If the new Moon stands on its points, expect precipitation to spill out.

A winter full Moon is a time for long cold snaps.

A full Moon in April brings frost.

Sailors agree that the full Moon "eats clouds."

Two full Moons in a month increase the chances of flood.

A pale full Moon indicates rain, while a red one brings wind.

A Christmas full Moon predicts a poor harvest.

The days following a new Moon or a full Moon are typically stormy.